Todd,

Continue to
Impact
lives!

Ann

Praise for *Live Life with No Regrets*

"We should all aspire to live a life of no regrets. Anne's new book will provide you simple, solid advice on how to do it."

–Mark Sanborn

Bestselling author of *The Fred Factor* and *You Don't Need a Title to be a Leader*

"Your choices and decisions up to now have made your life what it is today. This wonderful, insightful book shows you how to make better choices and decisions for the rest of your life!"

–Brian Tracy

author of *Reinvention* and *Eat That Frog!*

"Bachrach has done it again. These concepts are simple and straightforward, yet incredibly effective in creating the success and satisfaction that most people dream about. Entrepreneurs and business professionals either master this mindset – or stall out because they lack one or more of these essential techniques. Recommended reading for self-starters!"

–Dianna Booher

author of *The Voice of Authority: 10 Communication Strategies for Every Leader* and *Speak with Confidence*

"Would you like to be relaxed and at peace while living exactly the life you want? This book will show you how. Anne is an expert who lives peacefully and powerfully every day. Do it now!"

–Rick Barrera
author of *Overpromise and Overdeliver:*
How to Design and Deliver Extraordinary Customer
Experiences

"This is it, the ONE shot you have at being alive. Let Anne Bachrach show you how to assure that at the end of it, you can reflect on how you lived it and smile... from ear to ear! You are driving even if it's someone else's car much of the time. It's YOUR choices that matter. Take charge of your life. Love this life you've been given."

–Jim Cathcart, Hall of Fame Speaker and
author of *The Acorn Principle*

"A fantastic book about putting our busy lives into perspective and making sure we choose the path we truly want so we don't live with too many regrets. Anne continues to share practical content in a way that makes it easy to implement and get results."

–Naomi Rhode, CSP, CPAE Speaker Hall of Fame
Co-Founder of SmartHealth

"Live Life with No Regrets" is a prescription for personal and professional satisfaction and happiness. I feel better about myself when I follow Anne Bachrach's advice and I'm sure you will too."

–Lewis Schiff
co-author of *The Middle-class Millionaire*

"Make no mistake about it. We get out of life what we put into it. Anne Bachrach does an amazing job in sharing simple ideas on how we can achieve great success in all areas of our lives. *Living Life with No Regrets* is a must read! If you don't read it, you will regret how much you are missing out on in life."

–Ron Karr
author of *Lead, Sell or Get Out of the Way, The Titan Principle®* and *The Complete Idiot's Guide to Great Customer Service*

Published by

Seraph Publishing

www.seraphpublishing.com

ISBN Number

978-1-934948-12-5

Printed in the United States of America
First edition December 2010

Cover Photo by Erik Petersen
(www.ErikPetersenPhotography.com)

www.AccountabilityCoach.com
www.QualityOfLifeCoach.us

Acknowledgments

Thank you Bill, my husband and best friend, who always encourages and supports me in everything I do. You are the love of my life and words can't express how much I appreciate you and all you do for me, our family, and for so many other people. Your caring heart and vision for the future has and will continue to make a difference in so many people's lives. Your desire and commitment to continual improvement is an inspiration.

Thank you Mom for always believing in me, and working so hard to raise me and my brothers in a way that positively impacted our lives forever. I know it wasn't always easy and yet you never complained or let us know how hard it really was to ensure we had options to grow to be the person we were meant to be. You have always been a great role model for me and so many other women. I value our relationship and love you very much.

Thank you to all my clients who continually push me to create learning resources and tools to help others so they can enjoy an even more balanced and successful life. I appreciate you believing in the processes we use and wanting to share it with other people in order to also make a difference in their life.

I thank God for giving me all that I have every day. I am truly a blessed person. I believe I was put on this earth to make a difference. My hope is that this book helps those who are in need of what is written on these pages, and it does make a different in their life.

Anne

Table of Contents

Introduction

"At no time should you end the day regretting your actions or path. If you do, it's a sure sign you're in need of a change."

Valerie Latona

Shape **Magazine**

Imagine reflecting on your past, from any point in your long, happy life, and having no regrets. How did you get here? How would you like to free yourself of past regrets and live a life where you have no regrets ever again? What would have to happen from this point going forward for you to live a life of no regrets?

That's why I wrote this book. To help you choose to create the future you really want. **Regrets are a waste of time anyway, as you can't change the past.** So, let go of the past and decide to choose to live your life in a way where you will have no regrets from this day forward.

Living a life with no regrets doesn't mean perfection. It means you know how to make the right choice every time, a choice that you will not regret. You think about the impact and outcome of a decision and know you can comfortably live with the choice you make. We don't know the future. We only can make decisions based on what we do know at the present time.

Is a successful and happy life with few or no regrets a choice…? Is success a choice or a chance collision of various uncontrollable factors?

In studying self-improvement, we learn that we can't change others, nor can we single-handedly change the world. However, *we do have the power to change our own lives. We are living a life we chose, based on the decisions we made in the past and will make into the future.*

This is the single most important message in self-improvement. You do not have to settle for what you think is life's "role" for you. You are not doomed to live a life you are unhappy living. You are not obligated to do what others think you *should* do. Any and all of these self-limiting beliefs can be overcome.

You have the power to look for another job and make a positive change in your career. You have the power to seek out higher education to follow a different career path. You have the ability to define success for yourself and the capacity to achieve that pinnacle of success by working smart and exercising perseverance. Success is a choice that comes from being intentional about living your life with the highest probability of achieving your goals so you can enjoy what is most important to you. Success comes from choosing to live your life with purpose. This is how you live a life with no regrets.

You make your own choices. The choices you make will impact your life – positively or negatively, depending on the path you choose. Choose to live your life with no regrets from this day forward. You choose how and where to live. If you are unhappy with any part of your life, choose to change it – and start today.

If what you are currently doing doesn't serve you, you can choose to change it right now. When we change how we look at things, the things we look at change.

You can choose to start by taking "baby" steps. Start by having a day without regrets. How about a business trip where you don't have any regrets? What would a vacation without regrets look like and feel like? What would have to happen to have an argument or "touchy" conversation with your spouse or child without regrets? How would you have a conversation with a client you don't enjoy and not have any regrets? How would you communicate with employees who may not be working to your expectations and not have any regrets? Could you have a day of making everyday business decisions and personal choices without any regrets?

What would a day without regrets look like and feel like? What would a week of no regrets look like and feel like? What would a month of no regrets look like and feel like? Keep reading...

I Choice

"It's choice – not chance – that determines your destiny."

Jean Nidetch

Founder of Weight Watchers

1. The Choices We Make

"It is our choices that show what we truly are, far more than our abilities."

Joanne Kathleen Rowling

author of *Harry Potter* series

Let's begin with a game of fill in the blank.

I wish I had more time to _____.

If I had more time I would _____.

If I could have done one thing differently, it would have been_____.

If I could change one thing, it would be _____.

How did you complete the above sentences? In a dream world, what would you choose to do with your time? How would you spend your precious gift of life?

Interestingly enough, your choices in life literally determine whether your wishes, dreams and desires will come true. Dreaming of an Alaskan cruise or a trip to Italy? Start planning your trip and make your dream reality. Wishing you had followed your dreams and dedicated your life to animal rescue? Start volunteering at the local humane society. Do you want to be a scratch golfer? Figure out how much practice is necessary, who is the best coach to help you, and execute your game plan. It's that simple. You can *always* choose to do the things you say you want to do.

Life is about the choices we make and the impact of those choices. Stop and consider, "What choices do I have to make to be happy with my life?" "What choices do I need to make in order to live a life with no regrets?" Changing your life for the better begins with choosing what you want to pursue and how you want to spend your time.

What is the Definition and Meaning of Choice?
A choice is a decision to act in a particular manner or take a certain course of action. We choose what to wear, what to eat, where to work, a life partner, where we will live, whether we have children and

how we will live our lives every single minute of every day. Decisions, big and small, mark our journey through life, determining the roads we travel and the events we experience. Even choosing not to decide is in itself a choice.

You may have heard the expression, "it is the little things in life that are worth living for." Let's take that a step further and say that the little things in life can change our lives for better or worse. The choices we make in life, no matter how small, define who we are and what we will become. This should impress upon you the importance of making your own decisions. Your decisions define your life!

Continue to take steps forward, even when faced with a situation that takes you outside your comfort zone. Even if you take "baby" steps, at least they are steps in the right direction. Trying something new isn't always easy. Take action before the nerves have time to settle in. The longer you wait the more your confidence waivers and the likelihood you will talk yourself out of taking action increases.

Remember, success breeds confidence, so if you have to take "baby" steps to make it to your finish line - that's okay - just keep moving forward. Continue to accomplish little successes along the way and know that your confidence grows with each "baby" step forward. Before you know it, you will be beaming with confidence and that will show in everything that you do.

"If you want to get somewhere, you have to know where you want to go and how to get there. Then never, never give up."

Norman Vincent Peale
author of *The Power of Positive Thinking*

When in Peru, some people choose to hike the Sun Gate trail at Machu Picchu and others choose not to hike the trail. The people who choose to hike the trail are all different shapes and sizes, and have various levels of fitness. Some of the individuals wear hiking boots, some dress in tennis shoes, others have on hard soled shoes, and some even sport sandals. A few have walking sticks or canes.

- What determines who chooses to walk the Sun Gate trail and who doesn't?
- What stops people from experiencing things that they would probably enjoy – especially since they are there anyway?

- What do people miss who choose to not walk the trail?
- How did they justify not going in their mind?
- What was their excuse to choose not hike the trail?
- What could they have experienced if they went?
- What memories would they have enjoyed over the years if they would have hiked the trail?
- What memories do the people have who did hike the trail?
- How do the choices we make impact our lives?
- How do we make choices?

Logic Versus Your Gut Instincts

Many people believe that relying on their natural instincts or "gut reaction" always results in the best decision. Often, we just don't know enough to make a fully informed decision, so our gut reaction must take the role in the choices we make.

A Conversation with Mary Goulet

Author, Radio & Television Host, Coach and Speaker

You've written a best-selling book called *Go with Your Gut* and work as a "decision assistant" teaching others how to make choices they won't regret. Tell me how you got started with this.

I started working with individuals in 1997 as an intuitive coach. My business started on a word- of-mouth basis, as friends were referring friends for my services. During the first year, I realized the biggest issue for us is that we don't trust ourselves; more specifically we don't know "how" to trust our instincts and that became the basis for my book, <u>Go With Your Gut</u>. I had tons of material on the subject written and someone finally convinced me to publish the book in 2004. I've honed the process through the years, to the point where it is basically infallible.

What role does going with our gut play in the decision-making process?

We make decisions from three places: our Head, our Heart, or our Gut. Our Head is akin to our ego, our Heart is our emotions, and our Gut is essentially our soul, if you will, the place where passion, desire, knowingness, courage and wisdom reside. All the answers we search for are there.

The first chapter of my book is Don't Follow Your

Heart. Why? Because our Heart is not a reliable decision-maker because that's where we attach emotion and our emotions change constantly throughout the day. Our Heart is a better follower though, beware it will follow the stronger of the two, our Head or our Gut.

It matters not what you decide but how you made the decision. We make bad choices all the time because our Head and our Heart team up and lead us astray.

Our Gut always knows what we need to do, but most of us are too busy running our life decisions through our ego and protecting our Heart that we're missing the seamless direction of our Gut. Everyone has a mission in life, and that mission has a purpose, and that purpose is fueled by passion and executed through the desire to be of service. Everyone seeks to be of service to someone – his or her family, community, or on a global scale. That's the driving force for most people. We remain in tremendous discontent if we can't identify our core service, and the only way to know it or discover it is to go with your Gut.

Following your Gut puts you on the path to what

you're supposed to be doing. For me, following my Gut has allowed me to create a life that is personally and professionally very fulfilling. From kids to writing, to touring, to my radio show, I get to do everything I want to do. I don't have to think up my life, I just follow it.

Your Gut knows exactly what you want and is constantly giving clues and guidance on following your dreams. Once you start listening to your Gut and taking steps in the right direction, you will live your desires and achieve your goals. You can be where you want to be, doing what you want to do. It's all about making and trusting choices from your Gut.

How can people tell if they're going with their Gut?
Many people have experience with going with their Gut during critical decisions that must be made instantly, yet they have difficulty identifying their Gut instinct during less critical decisions. Knowing if you are making a decision from your Ego, your Heart (or a combination of both) or from your Gut basically comes down to language. See, each one has a signature language. For instance, the language of your Head and Ego

speaks in sentences and asks questions: "Why? How? What if?" Your Head is fear-based, wants to be in control, has an agenda, and is emotionally attached to an intended outcome. Your Head always thinks it knows how to get what you think you want.

Your Heart is the emotional place. If your Heart is making the decision, you'll hear yourself saying things with emotions in your sentences. Your Heart does not ask questions, it's more concerned about feelings. Our Heart's job is to fuel us with passion, not to make decisions or take risks. Our Heart is the place where passion, compassion, empathy, sympathy, and joy reside.

The language of your Gut is the easiest to identify. Your Gut speaks in statements or commands of five words or less, period. It does not speak in sentences nor ask questions. It won't give a "why" you should do or not do something. If the statement is more than five words, you just went into your Head or Heart.

If a woman were contemplating leaving her significant other, the language of her Heart would say, "I don't want to leave him because I'll be sad, others might say bad things about me and I'll be lonely." Her Head might say, "He apologized on bended knee and begged for forgiveness. Maybe he'll change his ways now so that I'll stay with him." Her Gut would say: "Leave him now" or, "It's over" or "Move on." Five words or less.

Why are decisions sometimes so confusing?
Sometimes people avoid going with their Gut by hiding behind confusion. Actually, when you say you're confused, you actually know what to do, you just don't like your options. So your Head and your Heart will stall by making excuses, hoping with time circumstances will change and you'll get to do what you really want to do.

The best thing to do when you're confused is admit your Gut. Admit what your Gut instinct is saying. Most people don't want to admit, "Yes, I know the relationship is over" because they think then they'll have to act on it. You don't just admit it then follow your Gut on what to do next. Perhaps, you'll do nothing for weeks or a month until the time is right. Knowing your truth doesn't mean you have to act on it this minute, but it will give you more freedom and courage.

When I want to talk to somebody about an issue I'm struggling with, I usually already know the answer and just need time for my head and heart to vent. I'll call a friend and say, 'Ok, I just want to talk about this for a while, even though I know what I'm supposed to do.' I give my Head and my Heart permission to complain for a while then I go with my Gut.

Are there times where going with your Gut is not appropriate?
No, because your Gut is the voice of your core being. Your Gut is always talking, repeating its five-word statements – guiding you to what you want not what you think you want.

I can tell when I'm getting ready to go against my Gut, and even making benign decisions, not going with your Gut makes a significant difference. They say God is in the details – well, your Gut is the master of details. One minor decision that you make with your Head and you may have just delayed what you really wanted in your life. For instance, imagine that you put off calling a prospect. Your Gut keeps saying, "Call that prospect" while your Head says, "I'll make the call later when I have more time," and your Heart

27

says, "I'm nervous." You finally call two days later and the prospect just signed with someone else. Your Gut really is the master of your life details and direction. Big decisions are easy, but with the little choices it comes down to where you decide from – your Head, your Heart, or your Gut.

If you listen to and follow your Gut, you'll never have a regret in life. The choices may not always be easy, but going with your Gut is true. If you go against your Gut, you will suffer consequence and regret. Your Gut knows what is best for you, because it is the voice of your Soul, your desire, and knows what you're here to do and what you desire in life.

Copyright © 2010 by Mary Goulet

No one is expected to make perfect decisions all of the time. Choices and deciding are not about being perfect. This is about making decisions that you don't regret in the future. Hindsight is 20/20 because we know the outcomes of earlier decisions. We know more than we were capable of seeing before. Perhaps we can learn from our past decisions and grow in our perspectives and understanding of other people. Perhaps we can make better decisions and choices going forward because we better know ourselves.

2. Choose Good Choices

"To live is to choose. But to choose well, you must know who you are and what you stand for, where you want to go and why you want to get there."

Kofi Annan
Former Secretary General of the United Nations and 2001 Nobel Peace Prize winner

Kofi Annan's wise words could not be more accurate. In order to make the best choices in life, you must understand four things: who you are, what you believe in, where you want to go, and why you want to get there.

Questions for Choices

The following questions can help you make choices that will take you to your desired destination in life. Consider the following:

- What is important to you in life?
- How do you prioritize the things in your life?
- Do your choices and actions reflect your priorities in life?
- Have you ever looked back on your life and wished you'd made another choice?

- What would have happened if you had chosen differently?
- What has to happen for you to make choices differently in the future to avoid further regrets?
- What kind of choices do you need to make to feel truly happy with your life?

The choices we make in *every aspect of our lives* shape us as people.

The Wheel of Life

In my accountability coaching practice, I begin the goal-setting process by requiring people to set goals for every area of their life using a coaching tool known as the Wheel of Life. The Wheel of Life is designed to help people focus on the activities required to achieve all of their personal and professional goals.

Using the Wheel of Life, people identify goals for each one of these eight areas of their life:

- Fitness and health
- Family and friends
- Fun and recreation
- Career

- Physical environment
- Romance/partner
- Money
- Spiritual development and personal growth

The Wheel of Life is used to help people create a specific game plan for what needs to be done to achieve their goals in each area of their life. With your goals in mind, you create a plan that helps you make the "right" or better choices than you would have made if you didn't have a plan. The Wheel of Life is designed to transport you from where you are now to where you want to be.

The Wheel of Life is used to help people maintain balance in their short-term and long-term goal setting. When one area of life is out of balance, life becomes a rollercoaster of high and low points. Our professional life might be outstanding, but our physical fitness could be suffering as a result.

Someone in perfect physical health could have problems maintaining personal relationships. By aiming to improve or maintain every area of our lives, we can achieve an increased balance and quality of life. The same theory applies to our choices. We must consistently make good choices in every area of our life in order to reach our full potential.

Note: To complete your complimentary personal Wheel of Life, go to http://www.accountabilitycoach.com/coaching-store/inner-circle-store/.

Don VanLandingham, CPA/PFS, Guardian Wealth Management shares: "Anne Bachrach has worked with me as my 'Life Coach' since September 2005. During this time, I have accomplished more in every area of my life, and I attribute that to Anne's coaching. I originally signed on with Anne to help me become more focused on my business, and yes, she has helped me do that. But the biggest value I have gotten from her is in my quality of life. My marriage is better, my physical health is better, I am more focused on the spiritual aspects of my life, my relationships with my children and friends are better, and I am just having more fun than ever before!"

You, like everyone else, have only 168 hours in a week. A person's quality of life is a function of how he or she chooses to spend that time. How have you chosen to spend your time, and will you choose to spend your time differently from this day forward?

Benjamin Franklin agreed, saying "Time is the stuff life is made of."

The Quality of Life Enhancer™ Exercise is a powerful tool to help you put your life into perspective and visually write down the things that are important to you in life and where you might want to choose how you might want spend your time in the future.

Note: To complete your complementary Quality of Life Enhancer™ Exercise, go to http://www.accountabilitycoach.com/coaching-store/inner-circle-store/.

Feel free to share this exercise with your friends, associates, and clients. Update your Quality of Life Enhancer™ frequently and measure your progress.

Career Choices

"If you limit your choices only to what seems possible or reasonable, you disconnect yourself from what you truly want, and all that is left is compromise."

Robert Fritz
author of *The Path of Least Resistance*

Most people in every industry could stand to make better career choices. From part-time employees to entrepreneurs to CEOs, the choices you make today regarding your career or business will shape your future.

Choose a 'Smart' Business versus a 'Dumb' Business

We make choices from the first day we decide to go into business, as illustrated by the difference between a smart business and a dumb business. A smart business is one that works at helping you get from where you are now to where you want to be and within a desired timeframe. You create a specific game plan for success.

A dumb business is one created with little or no thought or no long-term game plan that requires you to constantly go back and make repairs or fix it in order to achieve your business goals. In a "dumb" business, you convinced the "wrong" people to be clients and now you are stuck. Get out!

Too many entrepreneurs and other people don't have a focus and a game plan to execute. This is like throwing arrows with suction cups at the end against a wall to see if any stick. These people go in many different directions, without a specific plan, taking action after action to see which one will work. They just "wing it" and hope for the best. Some people are even proud of the fact that they "wing it."

Consistently "winging it" is not a game plan that anyone can effectively execute. What makes more sense: setting out to create your business right the first time by putting forth the money, energy, thought and creativity necessary to succeed, or going back and fixing it later?

At first, making decisions in new situations often seems very difficult. By identifying your ideal results and working backward to create a game plan first to achieve that goal is a very good way to begin.

Let's say you have already created a dumb business. You can forgive yourself and let it go. Choose to begin making progress toward creating a smart business. What do you need to do to create the kind of business you really want from here on out? Create your game plan – with specific steps – for what you want your business to look like in the future.

Choose an Ideal Client Community

Another smart career choice involves defining and marketing your product or services to your unique ideal client community. An ideal client community is the group of people for whom your services are best suited and most profitable for your business.

For example, my ideal client community includes business people and entrepreneurs who would be much more focused and successful if they had someone in their lives holding them accountable to doing the activities they know they need to be doing to achieve their professional and personal goals. A financial advisor's ideal client community might involve people who make above a particular amount of money or have a specific amount of assets, and prefer to work with a financial expert who can help them make smart choices with their money. Everyone, in every industry, has an ideal client community who their business best serves and who they enjoy.

The clients we enjoy are also usually the most profitable for our business. This is because our enjoyment usually comes from how much we are providing and helping someone and how they appreciate what we do. We strive to please these clients and in turn they usually do not mind meeting our price and doing more business with us.

Regardless of who your ideal client community might

be, it's essential to identify this group. Tailoring your business and marketing to the people who have the greatest need (and ability to pay) for your services is another smart career choice that will pay off in the long run. Typically, it takes the same amount of work to obtain a non-ideal client as to obtain an ideal client. Choose to create an ideal client community and save yourself the time, energy, and frustration of dealing with non-ideal clients.

To complete your complimentary Ideal Client Profile online exercise, go to http://www.accountabilitycoach.com/coaching-store/inner-circle-store/.

You have more experience and knowledge today than you had yesterday, so why not make good choices for your business every step of the way to achieve greater success with less effort?

Choose to be Healthy and Fit

"When you have to make a choice and don't make it, that is in itself a choice."

William James
American philosopher and psychologist

Have you ever heard someone say they will eat dessert (or fried food or something equally unhealthy) because they are on vacation? I have heard this so many times, I call it the "I'm on vacation mentality." Newsflash: calories don't know where you are or what day it is; they count just the same every day. The "I'm on vacation mentality," is really just a choice not to stick to your chosen goals. This is an excuse to let yourself off the hook. Like most excuses, the vacation mentality isn't going to serve you well especially if your goal is to live your life with no regrets.

This same rationale or behavior might apply to exercise. Some people excuse themselves from exercising when they attend a business function because they tell themselves they "don't have time." Again, this excuse is ultimately just a choice not to exercise disguised as "logic." Where there is a will and a desire, there is a way for what is truly important.

Other common excuses along these lines include the ever popular:

- "I'm different than the rest *mentality*"
- "It won't happen to me *mentality*"

- "My genetics are the problem and I can't change *mentality*"
- "My genetics are great so others should do what I do *mentality*"
- "I can't help it *mentality*"

Choose to Overcome Mental Obstacles

When you are on vacation, you can *choose* to eat well. You don't have to get sucked into eating poorly just because others do or because the menu lacks multiple healthy options. Prepare food that is healthier beforehand and eat that instead or ask for your food to be prepared in a manner that isn't unhealthy for you (i.e. baked and not fried or grilled with no sauces added).

We always have a choice and you can *choose* to eat well if you want to eat healthy. You can *choose* not to purchase things that are unhealthy for you and eliminate temptations. You can *choose* to eat smaller portions to avoid overeating or serve meals on a smaller-sized dinner plate. You can *choose* where to eat in many cases.

As you can see from most menus at most restaurants, you are not a pioneer in this area. Servers are well-prepared to answer your questions about health options on the menu and chefs and kitchens are quite accommodating of special requests. We live in a great time to be healthy, if we choose to live healthy.

In terms of portion control, make a fist. Look at the size of your fist and think of your fist representing the size of your stomach. Use this visual to help you with portion control, if you need help with the amount of food you can eat at each meal. When eating at a restaurant, choose to ask for half the meal in a "to go" container so you eat a smaller portion.

When you are attending a business function, you can still *choose* to exercise. You might even *choose* to skip a session so you can exercise. You can get up earlier, exercise during the lunch hour, or workout after a meeting. Maybe your exercise routine will need to be shorter than usual, but that's okay. Choosing to exercise for less than a desired amount of time is better than choosing not to exercise at all. The benefits of exercise are tremendous for your physical, mental and emotional health, even if you only workout for 15, 20 or 30 minutes at a time. Can you imagine having lived a life of no regrets without having taken care of your health?

Don't let the posted gym hours at a hotel be your excuse to avoid exercising. According to Peter Vidmar, an Olympic Champion, all you have to do is ask the front desk or hotel manager to let you in to the workout facility and most of the time they will oblige your request, even if you ask during a time that the gym is closed. Every time Peter needs to exercise and the gym is closed, he simply asks to be let in. He says sometimes the hotel will require him to sign a waiver, but he is happy to do it so he can get in his daily exercise routine.

Choosing not to exercise during a regular business day because you keep telling yourself you are too busy is just an excuse. Find 15 minutes to do sit-ups, push-ups, and other exercises right in your office. You can also take another 15 minutes to walk or run around your building or the block to get a little cardio in. Some exercise is much better than no exercise – get creative and *choose* to find a way to fit your workout into your day. There isn't much more important than our health. Being healthy affects many things in our day-to-day life. How we feel affects how we think and function every minute of every day.

Choose to Believe in Yourself and Shed Pounds Faster

The attitude with which you approach your fitness routine influences the outcome of your efforts. Negativity, including pessimistic self-talk, can dramatically affect your motivation to make healthy choices. A study out of Miriam Hospital in Providence, Rhode Island, found that participants who expressed confidence in their ability to meet their fitness goals achieved higher levels of success.

"People who have a positive outlook about exercising actually see the biggest gains (think sleeker arms, sculpted legs, and flatter abs) over the course of a year," Valerie Latona, Editor in Chief of *Shape* magazine, said.

The Miriam Hospital study, which surveyed 205 people starting a fitness program, found participants with optimistic attitudes were also able to sustain their healthy habits for longer. In fact, during follow up interviews researchers found that the participants who expressed the greatest belief in their ability to succeed were the most likely to be working out a year later.

While a positive attitude can help you meet your fitness goals and make the most of your workout, negativity can actually reduce the effectiveness of your efforts.

In her April 2009 editorial for *Shape* magazine, Valerie Latona related a story about how negative self-talk can affect her fitness routine. "Just yesterday I sweated my way through a tough workout while saying to myself, 'These weights are too heavy,' 'Ugh, I hate running on the treadmill.' Needless to say, I wasn't in a very upbeat mood. And not coincidentally, I felt tired and bored and ended up putting less than 25 percent of my energy into the workout."

To get the most bang for your buck from your health and relationship choices, Latona suggests taking steps to improve your attitude. "Vow to start on a new path today by stopping yourself when you say something unflattering and choosing to think bright, happy thoughts… You'll have more energy, and be in an altogether better frame of mind.

In the July 2008 issue of Prevention Magazine, there was a great short article under <u>Who We Admire</u>. There is a photo of five ladies who all have on t-shirts with a circle around the word EXCUSES and a line drawn through the word – basically meaning "No Excuses."

These five ladies were celebrating their 30th year of walking together. They walk every single day at 6:30am, rain or shine, and have logged an estimated 25,000 miles. They chose to change their life with what they can control so they could be fit and healthy. What would have to happen for you to choose a "No Excuses" attitude around health and fitness?

Exercise also has a very positive effect on your mental ability to work effectively and be very productive for extended periods of time. Studies show you miss less work and are more effective at work when you exercise.

According to a study at the University of Bristol in Britain,[1] people who exercise before work in the

---

[1] "People who exercise on work days are happier, suffer less stress and are more productive." *London Daily Mail*. 16 Dec. 2008. Web. <People who exercise on work days are happier, suffer less stress and are more productive Read more: http://www.dailymail.co.uk/news/article-1095783/People-exercise-work-days-happier-suffer-stress-productive.html#ixzz0X9IIpDD0>.

morning or during their lunch breaks are more productive throughout the rest of the day. In the study, more than 200 participants were surveyed regarding their attitude toward their workload, performance, and mood each day. The participants' responses on exercise and non-exercise days were then compared, revealing substantial differences in each area of questioning.

The research revealed dramatic improvement in employee performance, including:

- Forty-one percent of respondents reported improved motivation to tackle their workload
- Seventy-two percent reported improved time management skills on exercise days
- Seventy-nine percent experienced improved mental and interpersonal performance
- Seventy-four percent believed they were better able to manage their workload

"It's generally well-known now that there are many physical and mental health benefits that can be gained from regular exercise," Jo Coulson, a research associate in the University of Bristol's Department of Exercise, Nutrition, and Health Sciences said. "{During our study,} workers performed significantly better on exercise days and across all three areas we measured, known as mental-interpersonal, output, and time demands."

To obtain a complimentary health and fitness tracking spreadsheet, that you can download and personalize, go to http://www.accountabilitycoach.com/fitness-health-training-activity-tracking/

A Conversation with Denis Collier

Registered Dietitian, Certified Exercise Physiologist

You once made a choice to begin eating five foods that most people don't eat enough of in their diet. What spurred you to begin making healthy nutrition and physical choices?

One August evening, when I was about 10 or 11 years old, the boys in my neighborhood were in the midst of a baseball game. Of the many baseball games that we played, this one was shaping up to be the best of them all. My team was one out away from winning the game. A boy (not one of my close-knit group of friends, but an older boy who periodically joined us) hit a screamer right up the middle. As he approached first base, I could see that he was not slowing down and was thinking of stretching his hit into a double. That meant I had to cover second base. The boy and the throw from the outfield arrived at almost exactly the same time. I swung my glove, with the ball in it, backward in one movement and tagged him on the arm to record the game's final out and seal our great victory… or so I thought. An argument ensued.

"You were out!" I said.

"No I was safe!" he retorted.

The argument was getting heated. "Come on now," I tried to rationalize, "I tagged you right on the arm."

"You tagged me on the arm but my leg was already on the base!"

Exasperated, I pleaded, "That's not true! You couldn't have gotten your leg on the base because I was blocking the base!"

"And that's not fair," he screamed, "Because YOU'RE SO FAT!"

Those words ruined everything for me, and I don't just mean that baseball game. At an age when it was terribly uncool to cry in front of your friends, I could not help it – I burst into tears.

It was shortly thereafter that I began lifting weights. Essentially what happened was a negative *quickly was turned into a positive. Whatever the initial inspiration, I soon found new reasons to pursue physical fitness. At an age when everyone is struggling to find where they fit into society, I became the guy who worked out and watched what he ate. I reveled in it. Looking back on those days, making healthy choices was an enormous factor in my self-esteem. And you know what? It still is to this day.*

What are the consequences of choosing NOT to do things that are healthy for us in terms of our physical and emotional health?
In terms of physical health, the consequences of a life of unhealthy choices are well supported by science. Obesity, heart disease, diabetes, and high blood pressure are all conditions that rob millions of people a year of their health and well-being. The tragic part is that these are all conditions over which we COULD have direct control if we only choose to.

When it comes to our emotional or mental health, there is also good scientific research associating exercise with improved self-esteem. This is a key concept. I heard a quote once, "We can only rise to the level our self-esteem can bear." It is difficult to achieve great things in life (be it success in business, relationships, or health) if we do not feel good about ourselves. The cultivation of a high self-esteem is obviously a multi-faceted process, but choosing to do the things that put us in the best physical condition possible (i.e. eating right and exercising) is a tremendous step in the right direction. After all, everything we do in life can only be done with the one body we are given! It is best to take care of it.

What is the impact of choosing not to lead a healthy lifestyle over the short-term and long-term?

This question really gets to the root of the cause as to why people often choose NOT to do the healthy thing. The key is this – there are minimal short-term consequences to making the unhealthy choice. In fact, quite often it is just the opposite: the unhealthy choice is the one that is most pleasurable. This applies to many things in life, not just health and fitness.

Let me give you a personal example. I love reading. Two books I read recently are <u>The Pickwick Papers</u> by Charles Dickens and <u>Twilight</u> by Stephenie Meyer. As most people know, <u>Twilight</u> is a phenomenon, particularly among the teenage demographic. I read it, and I must say it was fine. There is no doubt the story is capable of grabbing your attention for moment – it is the kind of story you can read and not realize where the time has gone. In other words, the story is immediately enjoyable. Now let's look at the Dickens novel. The first sentence in that book is eight lines long. So is the second. And the book is 700 pages. My initial thought was, "There is no way I can get through this!" But I did – only through some perseverance and focus. Unlike <u>Twilight</u>, one cannot sleepily skim through Dickens and be entertained. But, all in all, in my opinion after reading both books, <u>The Pickwick Papers</u> is the far more rewarding experience. This is the reason why scholars are still *studying it, and people are still enjoying it 170 years after it was written. I doubt the same will be said about <u>Twilight</u>.*

The same phenomenon takes place with health and fitness. Few individuals can honestly say that eating a spinach salad generates the same immediate pleasurable sensation as eating an ice cream sundae. On most nights, it is immediately easier to go home and curl up on the couch instead of going for a workout in the gym. It is only in the long-term, after a lifetime of such choices, do the negative consequences rear their ugly head. My friend, who has successfully lost a great deal of weight, said it best when asked how he, an intelligent, successful man, could have allowed himself to go through life so obese for so long. "I knew that it was probably going to kill me; but I also knew it probably wasn't going to kill me tomorrow!"

The key term we all could benefit from exploring is that of "delayed gratification." We need to shift our focus from the pleasure that we will immediately get from the unhealthy choice, to the more fulfilling life of abundant health and energy that will surely come to us if we choose to make the healthy choice.

How do you feel about the concept of "living life with no regrets?"
I use a simple principle to evaluate the worth of any action: "What good will this do me?"

Not so long ago, I had an attitude that was only subtly different, but that difference was actually profound. I used to think, "What harm could this do?"

Let me give an example to illustrate the profound difference of those two questions. The value of video games as an entertainment source is always a topic of controversy. People actively engage in debates like, "Are video games contributing to the sky-rocketing incidence of obesity in our youth today?" Another popular debate is, "Do certain video games promote violent behavior in some susceptible people that play them?" Each side is fervent in their own belief.

My point is that these debates are not even worth having. A better question is, "What good are video games doing?" Now there is a question that seems more one-sided – it is difficult to single out any real "good" that playing a video game will do. Sure, we can debate if they contribute to obesity or violence, but it seems pretty clear to me that video games aren't doing much good, even if they aren't doing much harm.

Regret in life is like video games. In most cases, it is not conducive to any good outcome. The key is simply to keep progressing in the general direction of a worthy objective. The pursuit in itself becomes the end. It is impossible to regret such a pursuit.

How did the choices you made throughout your life effect where you are today?
I think I was one of the lucky ones. I always knew

what I wanted to do. Mind you, I didn't know exactly what I wanted to do, but I had a general idea. In my high school year book under "Future Ambition," I wrote, "To have a career in health and fitness." Now at the time, I had no idea I would become a Registered Dietitian, Certified Exercise Physiologist, and travel around the country speaking to people about how to use nutrition and physical activity to get "Fitter, Leaner and Healthier." What I did know when I wrote those lines in my high school year book was that I had better go to university next year. Furthermore, I knew I had better take physics and chemistry and biology because those were the first year courses you need to take to get into the program. My point can be summarized with a great quote, "Those who aim at nothing hit it with remarkable success."

When I look back on how I got to where I am today, I could summarize the process in three steps:

1) Have an ultimate goal.

2) Determine not every step in the process that will get you there, but simply the next step you will need to take to get there.
3) Choose to act on whatever that step may be.

What advice would you give to others about the life choices they make?
Try to find the greater good. The choices we make should, more often than not, move us closer to some worthy objective. Of course, nobody is perfect and this cannot happen all the time. It would do us good to realize this as well. The pursuit of the worthy objective is the end goal in itself. Not whether we succeed or fail. Someone once got me to do an interesting game. They said describe yourself in six words. This is what I came up with, "Striving for perfection while accepting failure." We can make the choice to do both components of that mantra.

To obtain more value from Denis Collier, go to iTunes Podcasts and search for Accountability Coach. Enjoy the many interviews with Denis.

3. Living Life with No Regrets is about Choices, and Choices Effect Your Mood

"In the long-run, we shape our lives, and we shape ourselves. The process never ends until we die. And the choices we make are ultimately our own responsibility."

Eleanor Roosevelt
United Nations Diplomat and First Lady

Choosing Your Reactions

Imagine this common scenario: someone cuts you off while driving and it upsets you so much that you hold on to your anger for minutes, hours, or even the rest of the day. You tell everyone you meet that day about the "jerk" who cut you off and almost caused an accident. Sound familiar?

Now envision what would have happened if you had just let the incident roll off your shoulders and moved on with your day. How might that day have been different? You can choose not to get upset rather than letting someone else affect your mood and waste your time reflecting on negativity. It isn't always easy to let go of negative emotion, but you always have the choice to create your own day regardless of what comes your way.

Have you ever been on a plane or other public place where there were parent(s) who were letting their child or children do what they wanted to do and not providing any discipline? What did you say or do about that situation? Did you just keep your mouth shut and sit there and get upset about the situation and wish the parent(s) would take a more active role in disciplining their child or children?

While traveling by plane for a business trip, I found myself sitting next to a child who was sitting in his nanny's lap screaming and causing a scene. The child even bit the nanny so hard she was bleeding. Where are the parents? They were in another row doing nothing about the fact that their child was causing a scene and disturbing everyone in the area. They chose to take no responsibility for what their child was doing and let the rest of us around their child try to deal with the situation.

Since I was stuck in the seat next to this very disruptive child, I had to make a choice: either be upset the whole three hour flight or try to do something about the situation. I talked to the child and tried to get him to think of fun things. The flight attendant brought a balloon for him to play with.

When I got up to stretch my legs for a few minutes, because of my interaction with the child a flight attendant thought we were related. I said I didn't know the child or the family, so I had to make a choice on how I was going to let his tantrums affect me. The flight attendants were impressed by the way I chose to handle the situation. They told me most people would have been angry and tried to get the flight attendants to intervene, but what else could they have done? We were on a plane and all the seats were taken.

I chose to not let this potentially very uncomfortable and stressful situation affect my mood for the entire flight or later. That decision got me through the flight and made the situation bearable.

4. *Choose a Life with No Regrets*

"We must all suffer from one of two pains: the pain of discipline or the pain of regret. The difference is discipline weighs ounces while regret weighs tons."

Jim Rohn

Author and business philosopher

How many times have you heard someone express regret about his or her current place in the journey of life? "I wish I'd followed my dreams and become a marine biologist," or "I wish I'd taken that African safari when I had the chance," or "I guess I'll never drop these extra pounds with three children in the house," or "I wish I would have spent more time at home with the children while they were growing up," or "I wish I would have listened to my mother," or "I wish I would have started school sooner." These kinds of regrets are frequently expressed by people from all walks of life.

Here's a secret for you to consider. Most people would not say, "I wish I'd done this, that or the other," if they had chosen to actually think about the situation and how the outcome would affect them in the future. If people would think situations through and contemplate the possible outcomes of their decisions, they can make a choice they probably will not regret. We are responsible for our adult lives. We can choose to do whatever we want, so long as we are willing to accept the consequences or the benefits of those decisions.

When we take chances because of our passions or we take action because of our ambition, we live with the results – good and bad. Yes, people can make rash decisions (especially when they are inexperienced, or in a hurry because of an unexpected deadline or other various circumstances) that have negative consequences on the rest of their life. Still, as long as you balance your future health and stability considerations with your desires for today, choosing to live out your dreams in life is rarely a bad decision.

Have you ever heard people saying things like, "I've always wanted to live in California (or go to South Africa, or exercise more, or weigh less, or work less, or spend more time doing things they really want to do)?" Well, what is stopping them? Most of them can do any of these things if they choose to!

Think about the daredevils of the world and people who live life "on the edge." These people get hurt and then climb right back on the horse to do something else that others might perceive as "scary." Some even die attempting incredible feats – and they die knowing they lived their life to the fullest. They did what they really wanted to do. They made their decisions and accepted the consequences or benefits of those decisions.

Do you think Evel Knievel is a person who lived his life with regret? In one of his final interviews he said, "You can't ask a guy like me why {I performed}. I really wanted to fly through the air. I was a daredevil, a performer. I loved the thrill, the money, the whole macho thing. All those things made me Evel Knievel. Sure I was scared. You gotta be an ass not to be scared. But I beat the hell out of death."

People who compete in Ironman Triathlons or other extreme competitions choose to do the work necessary to compete in the sport they love. Is the training hard? Of course. Challenging? Obviously. Did these athletes make excuses due to physical limitations, age, or other challenges? No!

Jack LaLanne, known as the Godfather of Fitness, says, "Dying is easy. Living, you've got to work at. You've got to have goals and challenges." At the age of 95, Jack exercises for two hours each morning after he rises at 5 o'clock. To learn more about Jack and his great story, go to http://www.jacklalanne.com/.

Take Vince Poscente. At the age of 26, Vince was a recreational skier who made a decision to take his love of the sport to the next level and begin racing competitively. Four years later, at the age of 30, Vince was competing for the Gold Medal in the Winter Olympic Games in Albertville, France.

According to Vince, seeing his former luge buddies racing in the 1992 Olympics sparked his desire to compete at the highest levels of the sport, "The sting of regret that I felt when I watched Bob Gasper march for the Canadian Olympic luge team in Calgary was enough to inspire me to take a chance and dedicate my efforts to make the Olympic games. I called it the 'Yahoo Theory' – if that yahoo can do it, so can I.

"Once I made the commitment to race, I called up a Canadian medalist from the Sapporo Olympics. "Jungle" Jim Hunter gave me the following advice. He said, "Have no regrets. When it is race day, and you have no regrets, you'll look back and realize that you did everything in your power to reach that point. This will help you during training; each pushup, each bench press. Each practice you run, you know that you pushed to do your very best. And you know, your best can be the best in the world."

"I thought about Jungle Jim's advice many times each day as it was quite possibly the best advice I ever got in life. I would be doing push-ups, and my arms would be shaking and tired, and I would think, "If you don't do 10 more pushups beyond the 100 you said you would do, you're not going to make it to the Olympics." I attached the idea of no regrets to pushing myself a little further past my goal each time."

Vince says that honoring his commitment to succeed was well worth the sacrifices of training. "I don't look at the sacrifice at all. Sacrifice is temporary. The feeling of "no regrets" lasts a lifetime."

The concept of living without regret has helped Vince succeed in his post-Olympian career, "When I started speaking full-time, there was zero demand for Olympic athletes who didn't win a gold medal and my effort to start speaking was met mostly with disinterest. I decided to apply the same philosophy I used to prepare for the Games to my speaking career. If I was going to be on the platform for a paid engagement, I wanted to look back with no regrets and be the best speaker the audience had ever seen. I thought, "why not try and be one of the top 10 speakers in the world?" Whether I truly rank in the top 10 or not is impossible to prove, but I aim for that level of quality in each speech.

"Success is a journey of integrity. Choose to do things that align with your values. Consequence will be what it is but the freedom of living your truth is profound."

What about you? You don't have to be a daredevil or professional athlete to live your life with no regrets. You can live your own "race" and experience the things you've always dreamed of doing or achieving. You can choose to change any circumstances in your life that are holding you back from living your life without regrets.

Where do you want to be and what do you want to be doing in 1 year, 2 years, 5 years, 10 years, and in 30 years? Make your life list, plan, and start turning the things you really want in life into reality.

Choose to Make the Most of Life
Happiness is all about choices and progress. We make decisions to the best of our abilities and then

move forward. The most successful people believe that they have a purpose and are destined to achieve that purpose one goal at a time. Some of these people face serious obstacles but they choose to overcome their limitations and are determined to live life to the fullest and serve others to the best of their abilities.

Many famous people have overcome physical afflictions to achieve incredible feats. Ludwig van Beethoven and Lou Ferrigno had to overcome deafness to achieve their dreams. Internationally renowned genius Stephen Hawkings is paralyzed and confined to a wheelchair due to amyotrophic lateral sclerosis, yet he is still regarded as one of the smartest (or most brilliant) minds in history for his contributions to the fields of cosmology and quantum gravity (not to mention his success as the author of the best-seller *A Brief History of Time)*.

 Never feel that you are limited by your imperfections or allow a perceived obstacle to limit your choices. When faced with a decision, ask yourself if you will regret any decision you make when you look back on your life. If the answer is yes, then you may want to reconsider your decision.

Choose to Overcome Your Past

No matter where you've come from or where you are now, your future happiness will be determined by the choices you make today.

In order to be happy in life, act wisely and forgive yourself for past mistakes and indiscretions. This sounds simple enough, but can be challenging for people who have high standards or people who have been hurt by others. Some people never let go of the past and choose to be bitter for the rest of their life. They may wonder "why me?" or have a self-pitying attitude that says they could have been happy or successful "if only..."

Rather than falling prey to the happiness thieves of blame, guilt, or regret, educate yourself to make better decisions in the future and minimize unnecessary grief and regrets. We can't change the past. We can make different choices today to create the kind of life we want going forward.

I once met a woman named Susie while vacationing in Mazatlan, Mexico. Susie was a happy, upbeat person who was clearly in love with her life. Her exuberance and joy drew me to her, and we became fast friends during my visit. She didn't appear to be from Mexico, so I asked her where she was from. She said that she had moved from Canada 13 years ago after she had fallen in love with the city and the people during a visit and decided to make Mazatlan her permanent home.

Moving to another region of the continent is a big step. Still, Susie said she'd heard many people express regret with what they didn't do in life, yet rarely heard anyone say they regretted something they had done. She was terrified that if she chose to stay in Canada she would regret the decision for the rest of her life. Susie chose to follow her dreams... and she's never looked back.

Susie's attitude and philosophy could benefit many people in this world. Have you ever not done something that you wish you had done? How can you apply Susie's philosophy to your life and avoid regretting your choices in the future?

As Mark Twain once said,

> *"Twenty years from now you will be more disappointed by the things that you didn't do than by the ones you did do. So throw off the bowlines. Sail away from the safe harbor. Catch the trade winds in your sails. Explore. Dream. Discover."*

Make a decision to live your life to the fullest. Decide what you want to achieve and choose to make your dreams a reality by starting today.

Actions for Living with No Regrets

If you could turn back the clock, what are five things you would change about your past decisions?

_____

_____

_____

_____

_____

Could you correct any of these items now? How?

_____

_____

_____

_____

What steps will you take to avoid future regrets?

_____

_____

_____

_____

II Choose to Change and Live a Life With No Regrets

"Life is change. Growth is optional. Choose wisely."

Author Unknown

5. Understanding the Fear of Change

"The key to change is to let go of fear."

Roseanne Cash

American singer-songwriter and author

To change is to transform or convert, to become altered or modified, or to pass from one phase to another.

When we speak of or read about change, the subject is generally that of a societal shift or other tremendous revolution; however, change can also refer to an individual's personal mission to transform a part of themselves or their life.

From the moment we are born, our body remains in a state of constant change. Still, the thought of change is cause for panic in many people. Why do we fear change?

We fear change because it disrupts our sense of security and consistency by challenging our perceptions. We don't know what's on the other side of a change, and for no rational reason we resist, thinking that will help save us from the jaws of the unknown. The fear of change also stems from the fact that change often challenges our belief system or "map" of the world. Let's face it: when the belief system your life is built on is threatened, that can be uncomfortable.

Whether you embrace change or not, change will affect your life. Unfortunately, resisting change only makes life harder. Inaction and resistance cannot completely stop change and will only lessen your personal growth and create frustration in your life. You will become stagnant and remain inside the boundaries of a very limited life while everyone and everything grows around you.

Reality check: change *always* involves a degree of uncertainty and discomfort. You can choose to face the change, take a chance and get everything you want out of life – or you can stick with what you know and settle for what you have.

What got you to where you are today probably isn't going to take you to where you want to be without some degree of change. Replacing what you've always thought and done with constructive beliefs and productive habits opens new windows of opportunity. Your thoughts, actions, and activities have to change to move you even closer to your future goals.

Do You Need a Change?

"Nobody can go back and start a new beginning, but anyone can start today and make a new ending."

Maria Robinson
Author of *Journey's End*

If you perceive that your current behavior is self-destructive or that your present choices ultimately will prevent you from achieving happiness and getting what you truly want in life, it may be time to change. The following questions can help you to assess your need for change.

- Do you believe a change in your life is necessary to achieve your goals?
- What kind of change do you believe is needed?

- Is your desire to change the result of a personal decision or the result of someone else's remarks or opinions?
- Do you want to change because achieving your goals requires you to do so?
- What has to happen for you to make the changes necessary for you to experience progress toward goal achievement?
- What has to happen for you to be open to change?

When you enter into change, you must believe it will produce the desired results. There's no reason to make a change in life unless your desire to change is sparked by an internal motivator and the change will result in you fulfilling what is truly important to you in life.

Change on the individual level can happen quickly, gradually, or over an extended period of time. The change may be the result of a conscious decision to act or a natural reflection of the individual's new external circumstances.

Change can be so subtle to be detected only by other people who are able to compare and contrast two distinct personalities, one past and one present. In other cases, the transformation is so blatant that the variant becomes impossible to ignore.

The minute you choose to change and take action on your dreams is the minute you change your life. You can either go with the flow that life directs you in or direct the flow and determine your destination. In just seconds, you can make a decision to alter the course of your destiny.

Some people say it takes 21 days to change a habit. I believe it takes a second. Have you ever decided that you were going to do something differently and just did? If so, you changed a habit in a second.

Andy Core has a master's degree in the science of human performance and has spent the last 16 years mastering the art of inspiring people to become energized, healthy, motivated, and better equipped to thrive in today's hectic society. With these credentials, this is probably why Andy's mother asked him for help.

Enjoy the story about Andy's mother who decided to finally stop smoking one day and then begin an exercise program because she had gained almost 40 pounds. She chose to change, has done many marathons, and did a triathlon at age 54.

Here is Andy Core's mother's story as told by her son, Andy.

As a healthy lifestyle realist, what I have learned is that there are only five categories that you must master to really get a handle on living a life where you can capitalize on the physical energy, the mental clarity, the focus, the innovation, the creativity, the feeling better, the doing more with less and living to tell about it.

It's simply how you choose to eat, sleep, exercise, handle stress, and how you choose to think. I believe your perspective or your outlook is the number one most important strategy in changing behavior of any kind, but especially when it comes to healthy behaviors.

My favorite story is about the person who was the least likely to ever live a healthy lifestyle, I mean the <u>least</u> likely.

This story is about my mom.

She smoked cigarettes, ate lots of Reese's Peanut Butter Cups, and drank large amounts of Diet Coke. She never exercised in her entire life. She worked in a high stress environment—cardiac intensive care.

Back in the days, my mom rode in the ambulances out to get people who were having heart attacks. She was stressed, never active, and smoked like a chimney. As a matter of fact, we called her a combat smoker. Whenever she would pull out a cigarette, it was like a whack on the side of the head because she knew what was going to happen. Her three athletic boys were going to charge, "Mom! What are you trying to do, kill us with your smoke?"

She would respond, "I'm going to kill you unless you leave me alone."

We'd nag and nag for years to no avail. She said, "I will never quit no matter what you say." Honestly, I believed her. But we kept nagging.

One day when I was in college, the phone rings, "Hello." "Andy, I've quit smoking." "Who's speaking please?" It was my mom. I couldn't believe it. I said, "Mom, anything we can do." But the thing was that she made the decision to quit. When you make a quality decision, the deal is done. She used the patch for awhile, but that wasn't what did it. It was her making the decision and she never looked back or smoked again. She had committed to change.

Almost five months later I was going to meet my mom and my brothers at a concert at Riverfest. This was a big, grassy pasture with people on blankets everywhere, an amphitheater, and a blues band playing with the Arkansas River in the background.

I'm just sitting there enjoying the sun and you know how something moves and catches your peripheral vision? I saw someone waving at me. I didn't recognize the person until she was within a few feet of me.

My mom had gained 39 pounds on her small frame and the sight wasn't pretty. As my mom sat down next to me, I felt like someone had just kicked me in the stomach. I looked over and said, "Mom, you have got to lose some weight." Pow! In reality, she didn't hit me. She didn't speak to me. I had really hurt her feelings. I wish she would have hit me.

Three days later, the phone rings, "Hello. Well Mr. Health, what am I supposed to do to lose weight?" my mom questioned.

I put my mom on a walking program five days a week for 30 minutes at a time. Why would I do that? Because exercise could cut her risk of heart disease by 47%, cut her risk of Type II diabetes by 69%, and cut her risk of many cancers by up to 23%.

That was the biggest win in my career. Every day, the phone rings, "Hello. I hate it. It's boring. It hurts my legs. I don't have time for this."

With the same compassion I said, "Mom, you're

being a wuss." Four weeks went by and there was no phone call.

Finally I called her, "Mom, are you okay?"

She said, "Yeah, I'm fine. I now enjoy my walk and I'm only going to say that once."

Three months later, the phone rings and my mom says, "Andy, I was doing my normal walk at the park and a woman about my age, about my size, jogged past me. Can I jog?"

"No! Are you crazy?" I responded.

Think about it, my mom, a 39-year combat smoker, never exercised a day in her life, now wanted to run. She nagged me until I said okay. That 30 minute walk now consisted of a 1 minute jog, and a 9 minute walk — 1-9-1-9. Every week or two, we'd schedule it down — 1½ minute jog, 8½ minute walk, and then all the way down to the day before her 30 minute continuous, non-stop jog.

The phone rings and my mom said, "I can't do it. I can't do it."

"Mom, you can do it."

Thirty-five minutes later, the phone rings, "I did it! I did it!" I could almost see her jumping up and down. I'm going, "Yessss!"

She now said, "I want to run a marathon!"

"Ohhhhh!"

Have you had someone in your life that has been so unmotivated, but then they start to get things moving, get that momentum, and then they become annoyingly motivated just like my mom? Have you seen that happen in your friends or family or within yourself?

Let me fast-forward my mom's story for you. My mom has since run 10 marathons! She deserves applause. She's crazy but... 5 of those marathons

*were fast enough to qualify for the Boston
Marathon.*

*She's run the Pike's Peak Marathon — 13.1 miles
up to the top of Pike's Peak, with a 14,400 feet
elevation. Do you know how much oxygen is up
there? None! And then 13 miles down with 125
other insane individuals. Then 4 years ago, my
mom did the Ironman Triathlon in Lake Placid,
New York.*

*If you don't know what that means, that's 2.4
miles of swimming in a small lake with 2,000 other
people at the same time. Everybody go! It looks like
a bunch of piranhas out there. After that, it's right
out of the water and onto her bike for 112 miles of
cycling through the Adirondack Mountains. Then
right off her bike into her running shoes for a 26.2
mile marathon. This took 15 hours, 58 minutes of
continuous exercise, all at age 54.*

Now there's something very important that you must take from this — that you should never, ever underestimate your parents. And you should never underestimate yourself. Once you make a quality decision and start building the momentum, the motivation comes for everyone every time. What felt difficult or almost impossible, gets easier and easier and more enjoyable. It can even become a part of who you are, what you do, and how you live. That's what I wish for you. That's what I want for you.

To watch Andy tell this great story, go to youtube.com link below:
http://www.youtube.com/watch?v=aRL3zeBBIZ0

Whether we change or not there will be consequences for our action or inaction. When we accept that change is a part of life and work to make positive changes we see the rewards.

Keep in mind that what you choose NOT to do is just as important as what you choose to do.

The Pros and Cons of Change

"There is nothing wrong with change, if it is in the right direction."

Winston Churchill
British politician and statesman

Some analysts have stated that when you consider "change," whether in the context of societal or individual improvement, that there are a few pros and cons to consider. Change can correct a sense of injustice. It can instill faith and hope in humanity and improve human relationships. Change can lead to better efficiency in production and lifestyle. Change can even save lives.

Some negative consequences can also result from change. Most people are of the opinion that all *intentional* personal change is for the better, but not all change is positive.

Once you set a change into motion you usually cannot return to the way things were before your actions. Altering the dynamics of certain human relationships could result in lost friendships. A person focusing on improving certain individual qualities might abandon their previously upheld values or alter their own perceptions of happiness and morality.

Choose to Accept the Consequences of Change

"Any change, even a change for the better, is always accompanied by drawbacks and discomforts."

Arnold Bennett
English novelist

One important aspect of change is the willingness to accept responsibility for the consequences, if there are any. When you consider making a potential change, you must ask yourself whether you can live with the results. This requires the ability to envision the possible outcomes of our decisions and actions. These considerations should include the affects our actions will have on others as well as ourselves. The possible outcomes of not changing or acting should be equally surmised and evaluated.

In order to increase the odds of favorable outcome, plan your proposed transformation. Resist behaving impulsively and make sure to create a game plan that has the highest probability of you achieving your goals.

6. *Choose to Become a Master of Change*

"For everything you have missed, you have gained something else, and for everything you gain, you lose something else."

Ralph Waldo Emerson
American Poet

Change is an opportunity for us to learn, grow, and expand our understanding of the world. Changes may be small or large, but each change brings the opportunity to learn something new about yourself and the world around you.

Every new experience allows you to become more adept at applying what you've learned to future growth and challenges. Change actually becomes much easier to handle over time because you gain valuable skills and experiences that you can apply to the rest of your life. Instead of being fearful of change, you may even have fun being open to change because you know your life will be better.

When we embrace change as the process of continually refining our perceptions and beliefs, change goes from sending us into a cardiac arrest and stressing us out to becoming just another task we successfully complete on life's journey.

Read on to discover how you become a master of change.

Understand that Inaction and Resistance Carry Consequences Too

In economics, opportunity cost is recorded as the cost of not doing something. In life, choosing inaction or resistance to change often carries bigger consequences than choosing to face the change head-on in the first place. Resistance just creates fear and frustration while delaying the inevitable. To quote the Borg from the Star Trek series, "Resistance is futile."

You are an ever-changing person in an ever-changing world. Learn to be open to the new and exciting adventures that change will bring.

Focus on the Desired Result

In order to follow through with a change, there must be something that inspires you to action more than the potential discomfort of doing the work required to make the change.

Do you want your end result badly enough? Are you going to do what is necessary – even when you don't feel like it? When you do, that is motivation. Focus on where you want to be when the change is complete. The mind has an uncanny way of being a goal-achieving machine. Your brain will create your reality based on the thoughts you focus on. Keep your desired end-result in mind at all times and only think about what you want to happen.

As Peter Vidmar says, "To be an Olympic Champion you only need to work out two times:
1. When you feel like it… and
2. When you don't feel like it."

Rationalize Your Fear

Fear is a natural response, but you should always try to identify what you are afraid of. Fear is usually the result of our mind creating hypothetical dramas that have no basis in reality. If you find yourself avoiding change because you are fearful of the outcome, ask yourself, "What's the worst thing that can happen?"

When you rationalize your fear, you diminish fear's power. You can just suck it up, and as Nike says, "Just do it." You might have even heard the expression, "Put your big girl/boy pants on and deal with it." Do what you are afraid of doing and reap the benefits. You will quickly discover that the experience of change, in most cases, wasn't worth the anxiety of the fear of change.

Break Change into Manageable Steps

For major changes, break them down into small, manageable pieces. We can be overwhelmed by the requirements of big changes and fall back or give up altogether. If a rock climber keeps her eyes focused only on the peak of the mountain, she can easily make a costly foothold or rock grasp mistake. When you know what you're going to do each step of the way, you have a better chance of sticking to your plan and get the feeling of accomplishment throughout the process.

Keep a Positive Attitude

Some changes are not initiated by us but instead happen to us. These changes can often interrupt our plans or even require that we alter them. The old adage of, "When a door is closed before us a window will open," is true. This perspective will keep us moving toward our goals. Looking for the positive in all events will keep us from getting dragged down by pity, anger, and depression.

Celebrate Your Victories

With each successful change you'll learn to trust your abilities more and soon be able to handle anything that comes your way. When you rationalize the fear and create successful strategies, you come out a winner on the other side. Look at change as a fun and exciting adventure. Reap the many rewards!

Don't be afraid to change just because you don't know how the change will affect things. As the old saying goes, "If you always do what you have always done, you will always get what you have always gotten." Explore what might be. Continually ask yourself, "What's the worst thing that can happen?" In most cases, the result will be something desired and good. Do something that you have been putting off and experience the results for yourself.

A Conversation with Jim Cathcart

Bestselling author of <u>The Acorn Principle</u>,
Motivational speaker

**You've achieved incredible success in your
life. Did you always know that you were
meant for great things?**

*In a word, no. I grew up in a working-class family
in Little Rock, Arkansas. Dad was a telephone
repairman and mom was a housewife. I walked
three blocks to school and lived in a typical middle-
America neighborhood. It was a nice childhood in
no way filled with poverty or threat.*

*I didn't expect to achieve much. I thought I would
grow up and get a job as a telephone repairman or
even a mid-level management position if I really
applied myself. In 1964 when I graduated, I
thought that it would be nice to earn $1,000 a
month someday. That was my goal. I expected to
have a wife, one and three-quarter kids, and live in
a little two-bedroom house in the suburbs. My
"plan" was to retire at 65 and die at the average*

94

life-expectancy age. In no way did it ever occur to me that I was anything special or that I would be anything substantial. It's not that my parents or education were lacking, but the notion of achieving great success just never occurred to me.

One day I woke up stuck in a dead-end job in a government agency in Little Rock making $500 per month. I was overweight, had no connections, smoked two packs of cigarettes a day, and had no money in the bank. I heard Earl Nightingale speaking on the radio in the next room during his 5 minute motivational program, "Our Changing World." On that day in 1972, the message of the day was that if you would spend one hour each day studying a subject you were really passionate about, you would be a national expert in that field in five years.

That message hit me like a ton of bricks. I was bored with life. My marriage and new baby made me happy, but my career didn't interest me much. I thought, "I've got a ton of hours – how can I do this? And more importantly, what will I study?"

I thought about my current job. That didn't appeal to me. Then, with no evidence whatsoever that it would work for me, I decided that what Earl Nightingale was doing on the radio with his motivational messages just "felt right" and that I wanted to grow up to be like him.

At that time, I'd never been to a convention and didn't even know that motivational speakers existed, but I became fanatically committed to studying self-improvement. I studied motivation, leadership, and self-improvement. I was listening to records, reading books, and surrounding myself with experts. I became involved with the Junior Chamber of Commerce (Jaycees), and joined a leadership-in-action discussion group.

With so much energy going into my endeavor, things started to happen pretty quickly. After six months, they made me an officer of the Jaycees and put me in charge of leading discussions. I got promoted in my job at the Housing Authority and was elected as the President of the Employee's Association for the agency. I started selling motivational tapes by Earl Nightingale and developed little training sessions to go with them, which led to another opportunity and then another. Within five years I was a full-time professional speaker. I met some colleagues and got involved in collaborations that led to books being published by New York City publishers. I've been the president of the National Speaker's Association and authored more than 15 books, and even earned the Golden Gavel from Toastmaster's International.

All of this happened without me going back to school, suddenly acquiring new talents and skills, or meeting a person who could open doors for me, and because I chose to become fanatically devoted to honing my skills in human development. Did I mention that I also lost 52 pounds and got in great physical shape? Today, at 62, I weigh the same as I did in my senior year of high school.

I am living so far beyond my dreams that I can't even begin to describe how fabulously different it is. All of that occurred because one day, without any reason to justify that I might be able to do it, I CHOSE to take the man on the radio's advice and devote one hour a day, every day, for five years to something that fascinated me, and I CHOSE to be committed to that goal.

How do peoples' desires affect their goals?
As Emerson once said, "Desire is possibility seeking expression." If you want something, that's an indication that the possibility of that happening lives within you and is seeking to be expressed. If you really want something, that means it's possible. This of course only applies to desire in a positive sense, as opposed to self-indulgent desire. "I desire ice cream," does not count.

Most people assume that if you set a goal, you have to know how to get it done. Nothing could be further from the truth. If you're setting a goal, you're saying, "I desire this achievement," even though the chances are good you have no clue how or whether you can pull it off. Goal-setting is the beginning of a process that reveals to you the opportunities that exist for achieving something you want.

For example, say you want a red 1965 Volkswagen in great shape. If I were to ask you how many of these cars you've seen in the last month, your answer would probably be none, even if you'd really seen five or six driving past. But the minute you write that goal down, you'll notice every car that fits your criteria going by, and if you see the perfect car, you'll track them down and say, "Excuse me, but might that car be for sale?" Before you know it, you'll have gone from not seeing any red 1965 Volkswagens to seeing one parked in your driveway.

How do you feel about the concept of "living life with no regrets"?
You should assume you're always standing in the light with the windows open. Assume that the

world is watching you 24/7 in all circumstances. If you adopt the belief that God exists and knows that you exist, that starts the process in a very profound and meaningful way. God is capable of being aware of you all the time. Any time you say, "Thank you, God," you're involved in a dialogue that doesn't involve a call, answer, or introduction. The last thing I do before bed, after saying I love you to my wife, on an ugly, painful day, is realize how much uglier and painful it could have been. I have all my body parts, I'm not suffering from disease, I can speak, and I can see. I didn't just lose my loved ones, I can read, and I can choose whatever I want to pursue. Wow!

Living life with no regrets means just asking yourself, "Later on, am I going to wish I had or had not done that?" For example, I was recently walking through a parking lot when I saw a piece of trash. I walked past the garbage, then asked myself that question and decided to go back and pick it up. People saw me go back and pick up the trash, and hopefully, that inspired them to do *something good too. I believe we're always paying it forward.*

If you do something that you're ashamed of or embarrassed about, immediately go back to the person who was affected by it and say, "I'm sorry. I don't like the way I handled that situation. Can we start over?" Get accustomed to apologies that are not about guilt, groveling, or weakness. Apologies can be mere corrections. A lot of people are afraid to apologize because they're afraid doing so lowers their self-esteem. When I apologize, the action has nothing to do with my self-esteem – I simply noticed my error and wanted to apologize.

What are the rewards of living life with no regrets?
For me, the first reward is peace of mind and a sense of being complete. This isn't to say that I'm done – I have a life force in me that feels huge and I have a lot left to do. I feel as if I've just earned my credentials and can now make my impact. Everything has been building up to the point where I can now just knock one out of the park.

There is so much living in my seeking to be expressed.

The second reward is that other people will feel your positive energy. When you are at peace on the inside and eager to grow and to live, others will take notice. Years and years ago, I read the Bible cover to cover and one passage that really stuck with me is John 10:10, which says, "I've come that they would have life and have it more abundantly." This verse coincides with the basic question as to why all of us are here. On the genetic level, the purpose of a human thing is to live. Why else would it exist except to live fully?

The purpose of my life is to live fully. I don't need purpose outside of me. I can find things that I care about and those urges inside of me tell me what to move toward externally. If I have a strong urge to travel, I should probably travel. If I have a strong urge to perform in front of others, I should probably pursue that.

If you're seeking your purpose, this is it: to have the most abundant life possible. Learn, give, live, and help others to your fullest abilities. To do any less is the physical equivalent of a sin. Why? Because if you don't live fully, there's no way I can get what you would have contributed. I think we are obligated to live as fully as we can live.

When I say that the purpose of life is to live fully, people begin tossing out excuses like, "If I had your money, connections, dexterity, or whatever… I could then live fully." But it's not about you doing what I do. Life is about you doing what you can for as long and in as many ways as you can, so that when you finally rest, you can do it with a smile.

Actions for a Life with No Regrets

Think of things that you have considered changing
but have resisted. Is there something specific that you
know you need to change?

_____

_____

_____

_____

_____

What will you agree to change in order to get where
you want to be?

_____

_____

_____

_____

_____

What are you going to begin to do that you have
wanted to do? Be sure to add the items to your Goals
Document or Prioritized Action List.

_____

_____

_____

_____

_____

III Choose to Eliminate The No Longer Acceptables

"If you don't like where you are, change it! You're not a tree."

Jim Rohn
Author and business philosopher

Many of us say that we're going to make changes and eliminate the things that deter us from achieving our goals, but few of us actually commit to improving the quality of our life. We stay in jobs and careers we don't like and in relationships that do not serve us. Worst of all, we often blame our circumstances on the "hand" we've been dealt in life.

If you have ever felt like this, it's time for a shot of empowerment and reality. Excuses, no matter how eloquently presented, are mere cop-outs that prevent you from reaching your goals. While some people will live their entire life believing they are bound by their current circumstances, you do not have to fall into the same trap.

We are created with unlimited potential but can be falsely led to believe that we are not good enough to achieve what we really want. Whether you were told you deserved exactly what you got, or picked up bad habits that sabotaged your success, understand that your life can change the very instant you change your thoughts – right here, right now. Whether you're sick of your financial situation, want out of a destructive relationship, or are stuck questioning the reason for your lack of spirituality, you have the power to create the life you deserve.

Changing your life circumstances is as easy as choosing your desired reality and committing to do the work necessary to bring that reality to fruition.

I repeat, "When you change the way you look at things, the things you look at change."

Creating the life you want begins with a choice to eliminate the "no longer acceptables" in your life. Removing the no longer acceptables from your life will create room for more peace and emotional space.

You will feel like a new person when you finally eliminate the things that have been holding you back from what you really want. Let's look at a few of the no longer acceptables that commonly plague people.

7. *Choose to Not Procrastinate*

"Procrastination is opportunity's assassin."

Victor Kiam

American Entrepreneur

Procrastination is a specialty for some of us. We have become masters at delaying the things we want or need to accomplish, even when completing the work comes with a reward. Is procrastination something that affects you to some degree? If so, why do you think we procrastinate? Procrastination can be attributed to several primary causes:

- Fear
- Perfectionism
- The need for an adrenaline "rush"
- Poor timing
- Mood displacement
- Lack of self control

Fear

"Fear stops a lot of people. Fear of failure, of the unknown, of risk. And it masks itself as procrastination."

Lisa Anderson

As Ms. Anderson so wisely states above, many of us procrastinate out of fear. This fear stems from many causes.

Fear of Success

Can you believe it? Some of us have a fear of success, strange as it may seem. We aren't sure what that next level holds so we hold ourselves back from reaching our potential.

Fear of Failure

Some people may worry about how others will perceive them when they fail, so they don't even bother to try. These people convince themselves that they are comfortable right where they are and don't want to attempt things that might result in a perceived failure.

Fear of the Unknown

Many times people procrastinate because they aren't certain of the outcome. They don't know how someone will respond to something they will say so they don't say what is on their mind. When you try things that are new and different, you don't know how people will react, but you just have to do it anyway. Do you know of any other way to be even more successful than to try new things and see what happens?

Perfectionism

Some procrastinators are perfectionists. They may start something new but stall because they view their work as imperfect and therefore that work is never complete. Conversely, perfectionists may procrastinate starting something new because they don't know the perfect way to complete the task or project. My husband, Bill, says these people are "getting ready to get ready."

I am sure you have heard of "Ready, aim, fire." These people often practice, "Ready, ready, ready..." and never or seldom fire.

Adrenaline Rush

Another common source (or excuse) for procrastination is the need for an adrenaline rush to jump start the project or work day. How many times have you heard someone say they work better under pressure or their best work is done when they are up against deadlines? Have you ever told yourself this? Do you wish you weren't this way?

Timing

Timing can also contribute to procrastination. Timing generally affects someone's willingness to get a job done in one of two ways:

- Overestimating the time left to complete a task.
- Underestimating the time left to complete a task.

Mood versus Displacement

Have you ever heard someone say they weren't in the right frame of mind to complete a required task when it was scheduled? Some people continually have the feeling that they aren't in the right mood or frame of mind to get the tasks required done. To paraphrase Mark Allen, six-time Hawaii Ironman Champion, "You need to do the work that the goal requires to achieve it."

Lack of Self-Control

"Procrastination is like a credit card: it's a lot of fun until you get the bill."

Christopher Parker

Impulsivity can be a major contributor to procrastination. Many people permit themselves to be easily distracted all day long rather than exercising the self-discipline required to focus on completing a task. Do you?

Delayed Gratification

In *The Road Less Traveled*, Dr. M. Scott Peck describes delayed gratification as one of the four cornerstones of self-discipline. The ability to delay gratification – meaning the ability to do the unpleasant work required of you before enjoying the reward – is a common trait among the world's most successful people.

Your parents likely strived to teach you the value of delayed gratification by requiring you to do your homework before playing outside or watching TV, or making you clean your room before you could have ice cream. However, many adults struggle with the ability to work first and "play" later.

When confronted with a choice between instant gratification and a difficult task, situation, or decision, many people choose to accept the easy way out. This problem becomes exacerbated when repeated over time. An inability to delay gratification can lead to denial and allow problems or habits to become worse as they fester with time.

In the *Road Less Traveled*, M. Scott Peck says "{The} inclination to ignore problems is once again a simple manifestation of an unwillingness to delay confrontation. Confronting problems is, as I have said, painful. To willingly confront a problem early, before we are forced to confront it by circumstances, means to put aside something pleasant or less painful for something more painful. It is choosing to suffer now in the hope of future gratification rather than choosing to continue present gratification in the hope that future suffering will not be necessary."

This idea does not apply only to literal "problems." Choosing and making a commitment to change requires one to leave a situation with which they are at least familiar, if not comfortable. The change may require difficult, sometimes painful sacrifices, but the change is made in the hope of future gratification. In other words, you choose to accept the discomfort and pain now in order to achieve your long-term goals.

Whining

Whining is another unacceptable behavior that can restrict your ability to reach your goals.

I had a friend who continuously shared the same problem she was facing every time we spoke. After several weeks of hearing her complain, I asked her what she was going to do about the issue, hoping that she would take steps to resolve the matter once and for all. She told me how she intended to solve her problem, and her solution seemed perfectly acceptable. Problem solved, right?

Wrong. Unfortunately for me, the problem was still at the forefront of her mind the next time we met for lunch because she hadn't yet executed her plan. I asked if I could help her by taking some action, but she reassured me that should could handle things on her own. Fine.

The next time we met, guess what? She was still complaining about the same problem! I finally told her that she had to take action to end the matter for her own peace of mind, as well as mine! "Please, let me help you solve this," I begged, "or at the very least stop bringing this subject up when we talk!"

Do you have people in your life who continue to let problems fester without taking action to resolve the issue? Do you want to be around people like this? I don't. Would you rather be around interesting people who have positive conversations or a person who is always reenacting the same old story over and over and over again?

You can choose to be around the people you actually enjoy and choose not to be around those who you don't like spending time with. (Although you may have to make an exception for family...) My husband, for example, has a personal goal to be around interesting people doing interesting things. This approach to life has allowed us to meet many new and exciting people. What would happen if you made this a goal for your life?

Whining is whining. Continually stating facts that are "negative" gets old fast. For example, even if the pouring rain is putting a damper on your plans, repeated complaints or commentary about the weather will not change the situation. Complaining to others about a situation beyond their control doesn't change the event and will only cause irritation and annoyance.

Rather than whining, spend time discussing things you can control and just 'deal with' the other realities that come your way. Others will benefit from your positive attitude and so will you.

Steven Pressfield writes in his book *The War of Art,* "The most pernicious aspect of procrastination is that it can become a habit. We don't just put off our lives today; we put them off till our deathbed. Never forget: This moment, we can change our lives. There never was a moment, and never will be, when we are without the power to alter our destiny."

Procrastination has become and is a habit for many of us. It is a habit that typically doesn't serve us well. It is a habit that can and probably needs to be changed to something that positively helps us fulfill what is truly important to us in life. Think about you and what you procrastinate doing. What will you do to help you not procrastinate in the future?

Defining Your No Longer Acceptables

Procrastination and whining are only two examples of the many no longer acceptables that exist in our lives. No longer acceptables do not necessarily have to be a general behavior such as whining or procrastination. You can choose to eliminate anything from your life that interferes with your progress toward your goals.

The no longer acceptables in your life could include other things such as:

- A toxic friend or relationship
- A job or career that makes you unhappy
- An untidy household or excessive clutter
- Compulsive spending or shopping habits
- Repeated tardiness
- A tendency to lie, steal, cheat, etc.
- A lack of education or training
- Vices such as smoking, drinking, or unhealthy eating habits
- A sedentary lifestyle (lack of exercise)
- Living in a city, state, or house you don't like

Anything that prevents you from achieving your dreams or makes your journey toward success more difficult can be classified as a no longer acceptable in your life. Once you've identified what you will no longer accept from yourself or your life, you must determine how to eliminate that behavior, person, or trait permanently.

8. Choose to Eliminate the No Longer Acceptables from Your Life

"At the end of each day you should play back the tapes of your performance. The results should either applaud you or prod you."

Jim Rohn
Author and Business Philosopher

Here are some practical steps you can take to begin eliminating the "no longer acceptables" from your life.

Apply the Pareto Principle

The Pareto Principle states that 80% of your results come from 20% of your effort. In other words, when correctly applied, 20% of your efforts can produce 80% of the results. Pareto's Principle, also known as the "80/20 Rule," saves time and energy while producing optimal results.

Apply this principle to every aspect of your life to evaluate how you're spending your time and energy. What you want to avoid (and this is a common trap) is applying 80% of your effort for a 20% return. This means you are essentially spinning your wheels for very little return or benefit. You might be surprised to learn how counter-productive your habits have been. If you find that you've been spending 80% effort for only 20% return, make some changes to flip the stats in your favor.

Applying the Pareto Principle involves making better choices with your time, money and effort so you can experience even greater success.

Are you swimming in clutter? The Pareto Principle applies here too. Eighty percent of your enjoyment comes from 20% of your things. Why not sell or donate the 80% of your belongings that are simply taking up valuable space and interfering with your life?

Do you spend too much time keeping up with what's going on in the world? The 80% of information you need comes from 20% of the things you listen to, read, or watch. Rather than reading every magazine, trade journal, or news story that you currently subscribe to, try to focus on consuming only the information that has the most direct affect on your life.

There are many ways to apply the 80/20 Rule to your life. Record how you spend your work time for a week. Write what you did every 15 minutes for a week. Now make two lists. Make one list for work that you could delegate or outsource and another list that no one on the planet could do except you.

You will usually find you could outsource at least 80% of what you are doing. Imagine freeing up 80% of your time! Consider reading *The Four Hour Workweek* by Timothy Ferriss to understand the power of this principle.

Learn to Say "No"
You don't have to take every opportunity that comes along, especially if it doesn't serve you or your goals. Which would you prefer – an acceptable job or a great job? How about an acceptable relationship or a dream-come-true relationship?

Learn to say "no" to the acceptable opportunities that only deliver a fraction of what you really want and "yes" to only the great opportunities that put you in a position to achieve all of your goals. Remember, you attract only to the level of what you think you deserve. You deserve the best, so start thinking that way! You can always say "no" to something now and "yes" to it later when the timing serves you and them even better.

Stay Focused on Your Goals

Always maintain a laser focus on where you want to be, even if it's not your current reality. The mind is a goal-achieving machine that will create a reality to match your vision, so envision a good future for yourself! You have unlimited potential and were created for success. You only have to decide and commit to accepting nothing less than your vision in order to make your desired lifestyle into reality.

Think about the impact on your life and business if you only worked with people who were best served by your products and/or services, your ideal clients, and not just anyone who can "fog a mirror". How much better would your life be? How much better would you feel? How much smarter would this be? In most cases, it takes the same amount of work to obtain an ideal client as it does a non-ideal client. How would you like to utilize the limited time you have?

Out with the Old, In with the New

Eliminating the "no longer acceptables" in your life is incredibly liberating. Once you create the life you want, you'll wonder how you used to live the way you did before. Choose to let go of those things or people that are holding you back from achieving true success. Make a list of the "no longer acceptables" and start eliminating them from your life one at a time. Once you begin, you'll find it is easier to continue because you will finally feel free to create the life you truly want.

You deserve so much more than you currently have, but it's up to you to earn what you deserve. You can accelerate goal achievement by eliminating the "no longer acceptables" from your life, and replace them with positive behaviors, beliefs, people, and attitudes that move you toward your goals.

Actions for a Life with No Regrets

Is procrastination something that is no longer acceptable in your life? If so, what will you do today to stop procrastination in your life? List those things below and just do what you know you need to do when you need to do it.

_____

_____

_____

_____

_____

What are some things in your life that are **no longer acceptable**? Write them down now!

1. _____

2. _____

3. _____

What will you commit to do today to get the no longer acceptables out of your life? Enjoy the benefits this has when you choose to eliminate no longer acceptables from your life.

_____

_____

_____

_____

IV Choose to Utilize Effective Time Management

"You will never find time for anything. If you want time, you must make it."

Charles Roberts Buxton

9. Choose Effective and Efficient Behavior

"All time management begins with planning."

Tom Greening

In the ever-increasing rat race that we run to turn business profits, many of us find ourselves suffering from sheer exhaustion. We spin in circles trying to create more hours in the day so we can check off all the tasks on our never-ending to-do list for life.

At some point, you have to concentrate on only the things that are important to your success and sanity. Time management is a *process* that many successful business owners and professionals find themselves having to learn and consistently implement in order to focus their energy on the most important tasks and activities.

Effective time management is not about figuring out how to move faster. It's impossible to create more hours in the day and it's simply not healthy to run at full tilt constantly. The objective of effective time management is to slow down and focus on the highest payoff activities that will produce the results you desire in the timeframe you want. If you are not satisfied with the amount of time you are spending on the activities that matter to you, reorganize, delegate, and change your calendar around until your time is spent achieving your professional and personal goals so you can ultimately fulfill what is truly important to you in your life.

Have you ever scheduled time for a vacation and before you left you got more done (professionally and personally) than you might have if you weren't going on vacation? How did you do get more done before leaving on vacation? Why not act like this more often? If you could actually get more done (and with the same or better result) in less time, wouldn't you want that as your new consistent behavior?

Many times, we do "busy work" to fill the time we think we have to work each day. What if you could get the same amount of work or more done in less time and still achieve the same or better result? What will you do with the extra time?

A calendar is essential to achieving your goals. If you do not already have a way to calendar all your activities, you need to get one now. You can choose a calendar system that is electronic, paper-based, or internet-based. You have many calendaring options from which to choose. Pick one and use it.

Scheduling all your activities in your life on a calendar will help you stay focused and eliminate distractions. In order to build your success, you must concentrate on doing the things that have the highest probability of helping you achieve your goals. Distractions offer no return and no profit. Your calendar should be designed to have the highest possible impact on helping you achieve your goals so you can realize your dreams.

If you are like many people, you will quickly realize that you don't have enough time in the day to calendar everything you want and need to get done (all those activities in your "To-Do" or "Task" list). This is why you must prioritize your activities.

Everything that you do each day, week, and month can be scheduled and color-coded according to activity type. This will help you to quickly create a visual picture of what type of activity is next. This includes showers, meals, drive time, fitness, professional, and social events. While this concept may scare you right now, keep an open mind and consider the impact of choosing to implement this idea in your life. On the other hand, consider the impact of choosing not to implement this concept.

Choose to Develop Your Schedule

As you work on creating your first draft of putting all your activities on your calendar, ask yourself:

- When is the best time to do each type of activity?
- When will I be able to achieve the best results for each activity?

(Note that this is a first draft of your calendar. Creating a comprehensive schedule that most effectively works for you may require some trial and error.)

Even now, I still have a tendency to overestimate the number of things I can accomplish in a given day and often run out of time to check off every item on my list. I think I'm better, faster, and quicker than I actually am. The reality is that I'm a very efficient person, though I'm not as quick as I would like to be. This frustrates me; however, it is the reality of the situation so I adjust my calendar to ensure enough time has been allotted for each task.

In order to avoid over-scheduling your calendar, make a list of every task you would like to accomplish and determine a realistic estimate of how long each item will take to complete. Remember to prioritize your list by putting those activities at the top that have the highest impact on you achieving your goals. Then add time to that estimate. If you are able to complete the task ahead of schedule, you can just move on to the next activity in your life (that you prioritized in order of impact on goal-achievement and your success.)

Once you have a list of all the tasks you would like to schedule, consider:

- Are the business activities that have the most time allotted your highest payoff activities?
- How much time do you spend or want to spend on tasks that don't produce the results you really want? Could those tasks be

delegated and taken off your list and your calendar?

- How much time do you have for your spouse or significant other, your family, your friends, your health, housework, and travel? Do you have an entry for date night, time with your kids, and extracurricular or volunteer activities that you enjoy?

Choose to Honor the Calendar

When you've developed a working schedule, the next step is to begin *honoring* that calendar. For many people, honoring the calendar is the hardest part of choosing to change. Many people allow themselves to become distracted or make excuses for not following their schedule. For example, many people don't think twice about delaying their allotted physical fitness time. If you find that your daily exercise routine (or another task) is frequently being skipped, you may need to adjust your schedule. Identify a time of day when you feel the most motivated to exercise and reschedule your workout for that time.

Choose to Train Your Team

You must also encourage the other people in your life to "honor their calendar." Make certain your assistant and other team members know that you abide by your schedule. This will not only set a good example for them to follow, but will also help with minimizing or eliminating interruptions.

Interruptions can be costly! When someone calls for you and your assistant transfers the call to you, that is a distraction. Your calendar should specify a time during which you return phone calls or e-mails. Have your assistant screen calls, take messages, and schedule phone appointments when needed. If you do not have an assistant, simply record an outgoing message that specifies the times you return messages.

You can also change your phone recording to provide a message that states someone will get back to them within 24 hours, and if this is an extreme emergency, they can call another number. Then choose specific times throughout the day (maybe 2 or 3 times) when you listen to your messages and respond accordingly. Your outgoing message could even ask for an ideal time to return their call to help reduce "telephone tag." This will reduce interruptions and distractions, and keep you focused on your highest payoff activities that will produce the biggest results in the timeframe you desire.

This practice increases the efficiency of any team. Instead of dealing with constant interruptions from team members, have them make a list of items that need to be addressed and schedule meetings at set times to review multiple items at once. Maybe you decide to meet first thing in the morning and at the end of the day to review items. Establish a system that works for the entire team to resolve issues while maintaining the highest efficiency.

For example, one of my clients works best with a four-hour uninterrupted time-block every workday. He schedules this four-hour window of time and honors it. His co-workers know that this is protected time and this arrangement works fantastically well for him. Discover what works for you and stick to your plan.

10. Time Wasters and Distractions

"Lost time is never found again."

Benjamin Franklin

American statesman, author, and inventor

Your income depends solely on you. The more efficiently you work the bigger returns you will receive. Take a moment and ask yourself where you truly want to be in your professional life and how soon you want to get there.

Now tell yourself how many things you did today, yesterday, and the day before yesterday that directly contributed to the future results you want. Then review how many things you did today that did *not* contribute to your success. Those things probably distracted you from what you knew you should have been doing.

What's the harm in the little everyday distractions? Those distractions are called distractions for a reason. They are keeping you from doing what you need to do in order to get you where you ultimately want to be.

Most of us would like to be and intend to be efficient, but few of us actually are because we allow distractions to break our focus. When you are working on something that you have listed on your calendar, you want to focus on that activity and that activity only. That means ignoring (at least for the time being) the blinking message light on your phone, the beep from your e-mail inbox, or whatever else might distract you. You can turn off your e-mail and cover the phone with a towel.

In order to achieve balance and success, the miscellaneous distractions that consume your time with little or no return must be eliminated from your schedule. Anyone who has a demanding career or runs a business has to consistently practice excellent time management, effective delegation and learn to say, "No."

What if it's true? Every 11 minutes you are distracted or interrupted by someone or something that takes your focus away from what you are currently doing. Then it takes approximately 30 minutes to go back and get refocused on where you were to then begin again. If this is true or close to reality, what would have to happen to not let this be true in your life?

It's possible to maintain the simple life while achieving a high level of success with today's technology. It may be harder to hide when you need a break. Your e-mail inbox is dinging, your cell phone is ringing, and your spouse or significant other is trying to call you on the cell phone because your office phone is busy. You have to filter the input to regain control over your life. No matter how good you may be with managing your time, there are probably "time-wasters" that can be eliminated from your daily life.

Here are a few examples of time wasters. Remember, it all adds up.

- Not doing similar activities in one time block can waste time.
- Spending time trying to fix things you can't and never will control.
- Doing things that can be delegated, or at least delayed.
- Getting caught up in reading all the personal jokes and entertaining things people send to your e-mail.
- Playing "telephone tag" when you really should work, as much as possible, by appointment.

- Entering into superficial chitchat when you really don't care and even sometimes when you might care.
- Going to meetings or attending membership group events that provide no real value to you or your firm.
- Letting team members or others interrupt you and distract you from what is on your calendar.
- Answering the phone when nobody else is in the office to answer it for you.
- Taking calls when someone calls instead of scheduling a phone appointment.
- Trying to make something "perfect" when it is effective the way it is now. It may never be "perfect" and you could be wasting valuable time trying to make it that way.
- Having a policy that you take walk-ins when it would be better, for many reasons, if you worked by appointment only. Of course, there might be an exception when someone has an emergency.
- Surfing the internet when it isn't a high pay-off activity.
- Spending too much time on all the social-networking websites when it isn't being used

to directly impact goal-achievement or someone else could do it for you.

- Checking voicemail when your assistant can do this or it isn't on your calendar to do.
- Getting sucked into "water cooler" talk, just because.
- Not hiring staff to help you achieve your goals. Staff can be virtual, part-time, and full-time.
- Getting ready to get ready. Quit thinking about something you think is beneficial to do and just do it now.

Eliminating the Time Wasters

Time wasters do nothing but impede or delay the ideal life you are committed to creating. The good news is they are simple to eliminate, if you choose to eliminate them. Time wasters, like the no longer accceptables, simply become something you used to do when you were okay with staying where you were. The difference now is that you are ready to move on and create your ideal life.

We are sometimes our own worst enemy. Knowing the importance of what is on our calendar, honoring it, and not allowing distractions to interrupt us is something that we all have to work at and may not come easily in the beginning. Give yourself time and make progress. You will find it will get easier and easier each day to minimize the distractions that hold you back from even greater things.

Learn the Art of Delegation

Many of the activities that take up our time do not move us toward our goals. Imagine how much more productive you would be if someone else handled all of your "low payoff tasks," leaving you free to handle more important matters.

In order to make the best use of your time, you must maintain laser focus on only completing your highest payoff activities. To do this, you might have to delegate certain tasks to others. Make good use of your assistants, team members, or other supporters like friends and family. Your children can complete chores and your assistant can handle non-essential items. You should be doing only those items that are absolutely essential to reaching your goals that only you can do.

E-mail

Aside from the phone, e-mail can be one of the biggest distractions in modern life. Checking your in-box first thing in the morning can reduce your focus on high-priority tasks. Coming back to see if you have any mail in your in-box twenty times during the day significantly impacts your productivity. Instead of checking for new mail first thing in the morning and every hour thereafter, schedule two to three specific times each day where you check your e-mail for a specific amount of time.

You can even set your "out of office" option on your e-mail to alert everyone that you check e-mails at a particular time. Here's an example of an e-mail response I received from a client:

> *"Thank you for your e-mail. I have completed my e-mail communication for today. As such, I will review and respond to your message tomorrow after 4:00 p.m. CST."*

The Internet

Have you ever logged onto the Web and found yourself spending hours doing various things, most of which you would consider not a great use of your time? Avoid getting on the Web as much as possible so you don't get sucked into wasting valuable time. If you have to get your fix, log on at the end of the workday or a set time during the day. Set a time that you honor - say, anytime after 4 p.m. – and don't get on it before then, unless you absolutely have to because it is related to your highest payoff work.

While we're on the subject of computers, it is a good idea to remove nonessential desktop icons. If you have a tendency to click on the Solitaire icon for a quick game, delete it. Out of sight, out of mind is a good policy.

Remove Desktop Clutter

Magazines you never get around to reading and the picture of your significant other taped to your computer monitor need to be moved out of your immediate and frequent field of vision. It's OK to have personal items near you, they just shouldn't be right in your direct line of site at your desk. Only keep those items that you are currently working on. Anything else can cause a distraction and slow the pace of your work. Keep only current files on your desk and file others away until you need them.

Eliminate Noises

Listen to soothing instrumental music if you feel you need to listen to something, but talk radio or lyrical music will distract you from focusing on the task at hand. Even alert sounds from your computer can be distracting, such as the sound you hear when you receive an incoming e-mail. You might want to wear earplugs or noise-cancelling headphones while working to see if this helps maintain your focus on doing your high payoff activities.

Discourage Walk-In Traffic

Set a specific time or times when you're available to talk and accept walk-ins and times that you don't. This will help you to focus and complete tasks more efficiently. Ideally, scheduling appointments (face-to-face and over the phone) is the most effective. If you work from home, this rule applies to your family also.

Establish clear boundaries for the times when you are not to be distracted, unless it's an emergency, like the building is burning down and you need to get out now. You might want to post a simple "Do Not Disturb" note on your door to discourage people from knocking and distracting you. Teaching others to respect your time is a win-win situation. You will be able to focus on your scheduled tasks without interruption and those around you will learn better time-management skills from your example.

Ask For What You Want

Asking for what you want is appropriate for all situations, but must be done with tact and friendliness. Busy professionals appreciate concise, focused conversation. You can show them you respect their time by not wasting it needlessly. Clear and concise communication saves time for everyone.

When you call someone, you can start by saying, "Hi Jane, I know you are busy so the purpose of my call today is _____." Most busy people appreciate you getting to the point of the call quickly.

The same principle applies when you receive a call from someone. You might say something like, "Hi Tom, What can I do for you?" This can help shorten the pleasantries and encourage callers to get to the point of the call.

Learn To "Cut Off" Excessive Conversation
Again, everyone appreciates productive conversation. If you find yourself in a conversation with someone and it's not progressing to a point or conclusion, wrangle it in so you can get to a solution.

Superficial chitchat is just that – superficial. If you would like to talk to someone, at least have a meaningful conversation to avoid wasting your time or theirs. Nothing personal, but most people would probably rather spend their time on things they would like to be doing, and those things might not include you.

You might even consider having some meetings actually be "huddles" where you don't allow anyone to sit down (unless they are physically not able to stand). Depending on the agenda for the meeting, these "huddles" are a great way to shorten the meeting time.

Choose to Work When No One Else Is Around

This can sometimes be the greatest distraction eliminator available. You can sometimes accomplish more in two hours with no one else around than you can in eight hours with a full office. Take advantage of alone time whenever you can without sacrificing the personal time you need to maintain life balance.

11. Choose to Avoid Distractions and Change Your Life

"A change in bad habits leads to a change in life."

Jenny Craig
Co-founder of Jenny Craig, Inc.

Breaking Bad Habits

Breaking bad habits can be difficult, but remind yourself that those little distractions offer little return, if any at all, for the time you've invested. Minimize distractions and you'll reach your goals faster – plain and simple. For example, if you're self-employed and want to increase your monthly income by $4,000, that won't happen by surfing the internet or playing solitaire, or allowing things to distract you from what you need to do to make the additional $4,000 per month.

Success is going to come from doing the highest payoff activities that have the highest probability of moving you toward your goals. You must minimize distractions and focus on the tasks that have a positive effect on your success.

Cathy Herrick Spencer's Story

Breast Cancer Survivor

At the age of 22, Cathy Herrick Spencer was the youngest and only woman to develop and re-gentrify the historic Gaslamp Quarter in downtown San Diego. A bronze plaque at the entry to the Gaslamp lists her name first among four pioneers of the renovation movement. The other three were middle-aged men. Cathy was just 30 years old when she was acknowledged by the Centre City Development Corp. for her award winning landmark renovations. By age 32 she was the largest owner of historic landmarks in the historic district. Always on the fast track she juggled career, marriage, and family leaving little downtime for herself. Her stressful life choices coupled with a divorce after 16 years of marriage made her take stock of her previous choices. In 1998, she met and began dating the man of her dreams. That man proposed to her in a gondola in Venice (the first vacation she had taken in over 10 years). She surprised herself when she agreed to marry again. She returned to San Diego jubilant and ready to begin a new and less stressful life with her new fiancé.

Within one month after her return from Europe, a routine annual mammogram revealed a particularly aggressive form of breast cancer at the age of 41. Cathy was told that she had a 65% chance of living that year. Instead of falling apart she embarked on the fight of her life. She made immediate changes in her daily schedule, reducing her work hours and work load and added more time for vacations, long walks, and quality time spent with family. Between surgeries number one and two, she and Joseph Spencer were married.

Two more surgeries followed in less than four weeks and then a toxic cocktail of chemotherapy drugs. Her two children were just 10 and 6 at the time and she was committed to the health and life-style changes that would improve her chances of watching them grow up. She often wondered if had she made a few changes earlier in her life, would she be fighting for her life now? Cancer was a wake-up call to put her priorities in the right place and thankfully she remains cancer free nearly ten years later.

Cathy's boys are now 20 and 16 and because of her decision to make a few changes and a lot of divine intervention she gets to be here to share in their exciting lives. Cathy and Joseph Spencer live in San Diego and together have continued to renovate several more buildings in the downtown area. They travel frequently with their two boys.

Cathy Herrick Spencer Shares

Knowing what I know now, the change I would have made would have been to manage my stress better in a variety of ways. One way would be to meditate and do more yoga. I already exercised with weights and was a size 4, at the time. A second way would be to have my priorities in the right place. For example, I would put my husband, family, and health ahead of trying to save everything I had ever worked for from being lost to my nefarious ex-husband in our hotly-contested divorce proceedings. As it turned out, when I told my oncologist I was fighting to keep my assets in a divorce he looked me in the eye and told me to "Give your husband everything he is asking for or you won't live long enough to win the fight". I called my ex-husband as I departed the doctor's *office and told him I would agree to give him the house, $250,000 cash, and half of all of my buildings except two of them. I thought I was going to have to start from scratch to rebuild my little empire but after our settlement I discovered that although my ex-husband could take away millions of dollars in assets he couldn't take away the recipe. I still knew how to make it and could do it again. As a result, I doubled my net worth within two years of my divorce by selling the two buildings he did not get at the top of the market and buying three more! It all comes down to making the necessary changes in your life that put your priorities in their proper order. Sometimes we don't think about where our priorities are and the order they need to be in to serve us better in our life until something "bad" happens.*

Actions for a Life with No Regrets

What are the things that distract you from staying focused on your highest payoff activities that you know you need to do in order to put you in the highest probability position to achieve your goals? List them below.

_____

_____

_____

_____

_____

What are you going to do to begin reducing or eliminating these distractions? What has to happen for you to put your plan into action today?

_____

_____

_____

_____

_____

_____

V Choose to Tell the Truth

*"Truth has not a special time of its own. Its hour is now —
always and indeed then most truly when it seems
unsuitable to actual circumstances."*

Albert Schweizer

German missionary, theologian and

1942 Nobel Peace Prize winner

12. Can I Afford to Tell the Truth?

"Honesty is the soul of business."

Dutch Proverb

Have you ever had an experience where it was
difficult to tell the truth?

Is the Truth Successful?

You might be wondering, "Can I succeed telling the
truth?" Not only can you succeed by telling the truth,
but you can thrive telling the truth. Telling the truth
can actually give you a competitive advantage in a
market glutted by people full of hot air. Most people
fear nobody wants to hear the truth, but they do! And
the ones who want to hear the truth will be your best
and most lucrative clients. Most successful people
respond to buck-naked facts, because most successful

people got that way by remaining grounded in reality. If you trust your clients and sincerely believe they deserve the truth, they will trust you in return.

The truth is the mark of a confident person who wants to have a good relationship with clients and friends. By telling the truth you will attract the "right" clients who can handle the truth and prefer the truth.

It's amazing to me how many people are afraid to tell the truth. The truth pays off! Telling people what you are thinking and feeling about a situation can be powerful.

One client of mine found that telling the truth strengthened her relationship with her clients. She was busy handling a lot of new business and she told a new client that they should wait to pay for her services until she was in a better position to service them – two months from now. They were thrilled she told them the truth and agreed to meet in two months when they would then pay for her services. Consider how the clients' trust with her increased as a result of her honesty and how many other people they will tell about her services now.

Can you imagine someone telling you the truth about waiting to take your money until a more appropriate time? How often does that happen?

On another occasion, I was working with a financial advisor who had made many follow-up calls to a prospect because they said they were serious about working with him. This prospect hadn't returned any of his phone calls and he didn't know how to proceed.

I expressed the opinion that if someone told you they were serious about doing business with you and then doesn't return your calls, you might call them one last time and say something like, *"When we last talked, you told me you were serious about working together. In an effort to help you make smart choices with your money, I'm following up with you so we can continue making progress on _____. Since you haven't returned my phone calls, you might not have meant it when you said you were serious and just didn't want to hurt my feelings, so this will be my last call to you. If you truly were serious and want to continue making progress on your finances so you can achieve your goals and enjoy what is truly important to you in life, feel free to call me at _____ (phone number) and I will be glad to help you."*

This response is polite, honest, and brings closure to the situation. Too many times we hesitate to say what we are thinking because we don't know how others will react.

Facing the Truth

What happens when you cannot deliver on your promise to a client? You tell them the truth and you tell them quickly. Waiting to tell them why you didn't deliver when you told them you would can make them angry and hurt your business. Be honest about the situation instead and speak honestly when you run into trouble.

After you apologize and explain (truthfully) why you weren't able to deliver on your promise, consider asking something like, "What has to happen for you to feel comfortable and confident enough to continue to have the same relationship we have enjoyed in the past?" Most people will understand the delay, assuming you had a legitimate reason, and they will appreciate your honesty. "Life happens" to all of us, it is just a matter of when, where, and how. We aren't in control of those situations.

13. The Truth Can Be Kind

Control your own destiny or someone else will.

Jack Welch
American businessman and author

Jack Welch, considered one of the great CEOs of our time, held the philosophy, "Tell me the truth and tell me early." If something bad happened and you knew and didn't tell him about it, you were fired. But if you came to him early and told him, "This whole project is screwed up, and I don't know what to do about it," you'd go a long way with Jack Welch.

Respect the Truth

Jack's respect for the truth extended to his management techniques. During his tenure at GE, the company used a tool known as a vitality curve to sort employees into three groups during an annual review process. The A group included the top 10% of GE employees, the B group was comprised of the middle 70% of workers, while the bottom 20% of the company fell into the C group. Employees in the A group were rewarded with bonuses, stock options, and promotions; however, those in the C group faced a different fate.

In one of his most controversial management approaches, Welch fired the bottom 10% of his company's staff every year. He believed that these employees were more likely to annoy than energize and had no place in his organization. Critics perceived Welch's treatment of these nonperformers as cruel and unreasonable, but Jack held his ground.

He once defended his system in an interview saying, "The best thing you can do for an employee, as soon as you know they're the bottom 10%, is to let them know it so they can get on, adjust their lives, and get themselves into the right game. That, in my view, is a kinder, gentler company than the company that winks at the truth… Cruelty is waiting {to fire someone} until they are fifty years old with a family, a mortgage, three kids in college, and a thirty-year stack of performance reviews that say he's wonderful."

My belief is that the truth isn't always easy to say and the truth is isn't always easy to hear, but the truth is usually better for everyone. Communicate the truth with clarity so that the person understands how it affects them in a positive way.

Fear of the Truth

Stop fearing what *might* happen if you tell the truth. What are you really afraid of? Chances are you will realize that what you're imagining is not only improbable, but not all that bad anyway. Tell the truth and let things go the way they will go.

Truthfulness and believability always have appeal. If you sincerely believe people deserve the truth and can handle reality, they will trust you in return. As Emerson said, "Trust men and they will be true to you; treat them greatly and they will show themselves great." The truth has power. If you tell the truth, you begin to play in a new league. You walk away from the games of "salesmanship" and into the realm of reality as a trusted professional.

A Conversation with Mona Santos

Registered Principal and District Advisor

Many people struggle to tell the truth, even to themselves, about themselves. Can you tell me about what your life was like before you chose to tell the truth?

My life was chaotic. I had poor time-management skills which resulted in me spending a lot of time focusing on things that did nothing to get me where I wanted to be. I was making excuses to justify my actions, partially because I hadn't really defined my goals.

At the time, I thought, "Here I am, this big, bad, self-employed business owner who is flying all over the country building a business." In reality, there was a lot of hiding going on – namely, I was hiding things from myself. I was having a lot of panic about business and experiencing moments of borderline despair, which is the opposite of my usual outgoing, happy-go-lucky personality.

What were the results of lying to yourself?

Lying to yourself results in being forced down a road that you never would have followed if you had only taken the time to figure out where you actually wanted to go. It's so important to tell the truth about what you're trying to achieve and how you're going to get there. If you do anything other than that, you're just kidding yourself.

Before I started telling myself the truth, the costs of my decisions were high. You tell yourself that you're working as hard as you can and doing everything in your power to achieve your goals when actually you're going in the opposite direction. There's a whole lot of denial going on in our society, but it's hard to get the results you want when you're not telling the truth about what you want to do.

The dangers of lying that your parents warn you about do come true – lying doesn't make you a happier person, whether you're being dishonest with yourself or others.

What happened when you began telling the truth?

Telling the truth about a situation is terrifying yet invigorating at the same time. In a word, telling the truth is scary. It is quite an awakening when you look at your life and realize that you haven't been telling the truth about what you want and what you're doing (or not doing) to get there. You have the realization that you have to reinvent yourself because you're standing in your own way.

Sometimes telling the truth takes tremendous will-power. There are times when I look at a situation and think, "I don't want to face this right now," but lying about a situation in order to avoid it gets you nowhere.

How does telling the truth affect the choices you make?

Some of my earlier decisions were certainly made without a lot of reflection about what I really wanted. Before I started being honest with myself, a lot of my decisions were made without any real strategy. I made many choices that were doing nothing but repeating the insanity I was living in. In a sense, not telling the truth led to me not making the decisions I needed to make to move forward.

Now that I am honest with myself about my life and my business, I know that every day I have a choice of what I have to do with my time and I can either choose to use that time to bring me closer to my goals or not.

What advice would you offer to others about the life choices they make?

I would advise people to start at the beginning and determine what they are trying to achieve in the first place. If you haven't figured out what you're trying to achieve, what's the point? Be truthful with yourself about whether you're doing what you need to do to get where you need to be. And then you have to be honest about whether you're really willing to do the work and put in the time necessary to get there.

You have to be honest with and accountable to yourself if you want to achieve your goals. However, I don't really believe anyone is capable of being accountable to themselves all the time. In my experience, it's the day-to-day decisions that often get out of control – larger life decisions are pretty well thought through, but with the smaller decision it becomes harder to stay focused. Emotions and laziness get in the way of consistently making the right choices about what to do with your time and your life. Sometimes you get tired and you don't want to have to work all the time. Those feelings and emotions can cause you to kid yourself – even lie to yourself – in ways you can't even imagine.

Everybody needs some form of reality check in life because sometimes, "Am I telling the truth?" is a hard question to ask yourself and an even harder question to answer. Everyone should have some form of coach (even if it's their mother) – someone who will tell the truth, help them acknowledge the truth, and help them determine what the truth is for them.

How do you feel about the concept of "living life with no regrets"?

Living with no regrets seems like a pretty pleasing way to live. I think that, in a way, I already do embrace a life without regrets because when I look at my life, I realize that if I had chosen to do things differently, I wouldn't be where I am now.

Living without regrets is probably one of the highest levels of personal evolution that you can achieve. When you can look back and say, "I would not have done anything differently," you've reached a powerful place in your life.

Actions for a Life with No Regrets

What truth will you say to someone that you have wanted to say but were afraid to say before?

_____

_____

_____

_____

_____

What truths will you commit to communicating more consistently?

_____

_____

_____

_____

What results do you hope occur by telling the truth? What do you hope to learn or find out as a result of your honesty?

_____

_____

_____

_____

VI Choose to Make Commitments

"The quality of a person's life is in direct proportion to their commitment to excellence, regardless of their chosen field of endeavor."

Vince Lombardi
American football coach

14. Commitment

"Commitment unlocks the doors of imagination, allows vision, and gives us the "right stuff" to turn our dreams into reality."

James Womack
Author

If the previous chapters have inspired you to make better choices and bring about changes in your life, you're on the way to a better, brighter future. Unfortunately, simply choosing to change is not enough. You must commit to your new lifestyle and honor that commitment to your future self.

Commitment is sticking by your word or course of action, even when it would be easier to do otherwise.

When you commit to something, you make a pledge that you will do what you said you would do. Committing to something might require that you delay gratification and make a choice to forgo immediate pleasure for future gain.

Commitment Defined

commitment [kuh-mit-muhnt] – noun
the state of being bound emotionally or intellectually to a course of action or to another person or persons

If you do not commit to realizing the goals and life choices you have made for yourself, those lofty objectives will remain as mere fleeting desires that time will erase from your memory. It's easy to decide you want to lose 10 pounds, spend more time with your family, or cultivate better client relationships; however, if you do not *commit* to those goals, your choices become irrelevant because they never become reality. Commitment is the glue that holds it all together.

When you think of commitment, the expression "actions speak louder than words" might spring to your mind. Most people have no problem saying they are going to do better, but a far smaller group of people can successfully commit to raising their level of performance and then actually execute the actions required to reach that goal. You want to be in this group.

Without commitment, most people will quickly find that the gap between their intentions and their actions is too vast. No matter how nice a choice or goal sounds in theory, most people struggle to fulfill their intentions and actually take the steps necessary to achieve the goal. Commitment bridges the divide between our intentions and our actions.

Choose Follow-Through Versus Failure

Commitment is the foundation of *follow-through,* which is an essential criterion for goal achievement. Follow-through can be defined as "consistently performing each of the actions or behaviors required to achieve a goal in the desired time frame." Notice there are two main elements of proper follow-through:

- Completing the action steps required to accomplish an objective
- Consistently performing these steps in a timely manner

Identifying the action steps to move forward is simple. If you want to lose weight, start with reducing your calorie consumption and begin incorporating exercise into your regular routine. The challenge is not found in defining the goal or necessary action steps, but in actually following through and changing the problem behavior or implementing a new habit. Are you able to follow through with your goal at decision time? Can you commit to your weight loss goal and actually choose the healthy option from the menu when you're at a celebration dinner with your friend? Are you able to push yourself to hit the gym after a long day at the office? If you cannot follow through on your commitment to yourself by modifying these behaviors, you will never achieve the goal. Go to http://www.accountabilitycoach.com/fitness-health-training-activity-tracking/ if you would like a complimentary Health and Fitness Tracking Spreadsheet template to download and customize for your personal use.

Writing Out Rain Checks

"There's a difference between interest and commitment. When you're interested in doing something, you do it only

when circumstances permit. When you're committed to something, you accept no excuses, only results."

Art Turock
Motivational Speaker

Some people get ready to do the work they need to do, only to make excuses and give themselves a rain check to do the activity later. They let themselves off the hook for the gym after a stressful day at work or indulge in a calorie-rich meal because it's convenient. They say, "I'll make it up next time," and they proceed to behave in a manner that is inconsistent with goal achievement.

For a while, people allow themselves to buy the "next time" excuse and truly believe that they'll complete the activity or make a better choice in the future when the circumstances are better. Eventually though, the brain realizes that "next time" is never going to arrive and stops issuing reminders to do the work. "Next time" becomes never, and the goal falls by the wayside.

Poor follow-through is a problem that will affect virtually every aspect of your life. The inability to follow through and commit to doing the work required to achieve a goal will prevent you from reaching your potential in your personal, financial, relational, and career life. If you are serious about making changes to live a life without regrets, honing your commitment skills and developing the ability to follow through with your goals becomes critical.

Making a commitment to something becomes easier when you've developed key character traits, beliefs, and behaviors.

The truth is, making a successful commitment is nothing more than a making a choice to create a desired future outcome. You may say that people who stick to their commitments are an exception, but the ability to make a commitment is not personality-specific. Each of us is capable of making and meeting successful commitments. Here are five tips in making successful commitments that produce results.

1) Commitment is Nothing More Than Choice

By committing, you are choosing your desired future outcome over your current reality. If you really want to lose weight, then you choose to be fit. If you really want to save money for a down-payment on a house, then you choose to budget. That's it – you just made a choice! The chocolate cake and new shoes didn't even enter your mind because they aren't what you really want. What you really want is to be fit, or to own your own home. Once you choose your desired future outcome, you remove (or at least reduce) the struggle that leads to exceptions.

2) Instant Gratification vs. Future Outcome

Do you want your new home or those new shoes? Successful commitment relies on the individual steps between your current reality and your goal. Make every step count, and you will get there faster and easier. Focus on your future goal and outcome and why it means more to you than a fleeting desire for instant gratification. By holding your future clear in your mind, you will make the right decisions to support your goals.

Think about how you will feel when you achieve the future goal and outcome. What are two or three words that describe how you will feel?

3) Success Relies on 100% Commitment

It's easy to make excuses and exceptions, but it's harder to get back on track once you've made room for them. Successful goal achievement requires 100% commitment. Not 99%, not even 99.9%. Making exceptions sets you up for failure and makes it harder to stay on track. Decide what you can commit to and stick to it – no excuses, no exceptions. You'll find that 100% commitment is actually easier than 99.9%, because you remove distractions and the emotion around them. When you can focus solely on your goal, not your distractions, it will be easier to stay on track.

4) Casual Interest or Complete Dedication

You might be interested in the study of law, but are you committed to becoming a lawyer? You might be interested in losing weight, but are you committed to being fit and healthy? You might be interested in saving money for a down-payment on a house, but are you committed to a budget? These are all questions to ask when committing to a goal. Your level of desire will determine your results – period. If you only have an interest in something, sticking to your plan will be a challenge. However, if you really want something, you will be truly committed to creating it.

5) Visualize Your Goal

Visualization is a powerful tool that will support your efforts. Spend a few moments every day, in the morning and evening, visualizing your desired outcome. When you make a call, what do you want the client or prospect to say? For each activity you do

169

every day, what is the result you want to achieve? Imagine it as if you were already there. Feel how good you feel and completely immerse yourself in the emotions, smell, and sounds of the activity and the environment. Visualize what you really want and that will increase the probability of it actually happening. When you are able to focus on the end result instead of momentary temptation, you will make the right choices that support your desired outcome.

If you've tried and failed in past commitments, it doesn't matter. The past is the past and you are a different person today. Starting right now you are now armed with the strength and the tools you need to successfully commit to creating your desired future outcome. Never give up.

15. Choose to Unlock the Power of Persistence

"I will persist until I succeed. Always will I take another step. If that is of no avail I will take another, and yet another. In truth, one step at a time is not too difficult... I know that small attempts, repeated, will complete any undertaking."

Og Mandino

Author of *The Greatest Salesman in the World*

Persistence is defined as the "the act of persevering" or "continuing or repeating behavior". The most successful people in life are always persistent. They continue to work toward their goals even when that is not the easiest choice. Persistence is closely related to commitment and perseverance. This is why it is important to cultivate the quality of persistence no matter what you are aiming to achieve in your life.

Without cultivating the quality of persistence, there is not much for a person to do in the world besides become a follower and allow him or herself to be controlled by the wisdom (and/or stupidity) of others. Persistent people make the world turn — they make business grow, they improve worldwide communication, and they help to shape this generation's zeitgeist. Persistent people make the impossible possible and drive success and innovation forward.

Persistence Pays Off

Spirituality

Persistence is important for building faith or adding value to a chosen belief system. Religious-minded people rely on persistence to build trust with God, just as atheists and agonistics support their beliefs by persistently seeking out scientific evidence to validate their claims. Most every belief system in existence is based on a persistent and deliberate influx of knowledge and experience. To develop a relationship with a higher power, people must be persistent and persevere in developing their faith.

Persistence in Business

Professionally-speaking, persistence is one of the most important character traits a person can have. New business owners are often-times singular proponents of their company and must work twice as hard to establish a market share and brand their name in the minds of prospective clients. This requires persistence as there could be many slow months to start with and plenty of uninterested people... in the beginning. Persistence is vital if your goal is to succeed in a business.

Overcoming Rejection

Persistence is also an important quality for professionals to learn since rejection and criticism are prevalent in many fields. Take the entertainment industry as an example. Writers and artists must read rejection slips while actors and singers could be turned away immediately after an audition. This is just part of the business. Other industries are just as competitive and require persistence to survive office politics, job promotions, business development, managerial responsibilities, and corporate takeovers. Even when the odds seem stacked against you, it's critical to persevere toward your goals. Anything else will result in failure.

There was a time when I promoted my husband as a professional speaker. Like many industries, the speaking business comes with a lot of rejection. I had to be persistent to get phone appointments with decision-makers who could hire him to speak at their conventions. I would call people until they would talk to me or ask me not to call back (thank goodness this didn't happen often).

As a result of my persistence, I was able to schedule many speaking engagements with prestigious organizations and event coordinators. Many of the executives that agreed to bring my husband in to speak commented that they wished the people in their organization were as persistent as I was because they could have acquired more business and become even more successful.

Persistent or Just Plain Pesky?

Persistence is not always looked upon favorably because of the negative connotations associated with its close relative: pesky.

What really is the difference between being persistent and being a royal pain in the butt? Persistence must always have a purpose. Persistence requires a great degree of premeditated thought and advanced planning. When someone is persistent, they are fully committed, not to an action, but to a plan. There is a huge distinction between being committed to repeating a behavior indefinitely for no distinct purpose and being commitment to performing the behaviors required of a plan.

Successful people believe in a principle and realize that persistence will be required in order to achieve their goals. Someone who is merely pesky uses this repetitive technique as an offensive attack and does so until someone else has the courage to shut them up. Persistence is a far more appealing approach. A persistent person realizes the importance of repetition but is careful about proper timing and using appropriate language. You could say that a persistent person is careful to create a plan of action and then stick to that plan. When problems or issues are discovered, the persistent mind creates alternative routes and adaptable strategies. A truly persistent person allows nothing to stand between themselves and their goals. They have a belief system that benefits them.

Choose to Celebrate Your Victories

Another way to develop your commitment to your goals is to succeed. Success should not only be celebrated at the finish line, but along every milestone of the goal. People are excited by the rush of successfully completing an endeavor – the feeling that they get when they work hard to accomplish something and achieve the desired results. Simply taking the time to celebrate your successes and congratulate yourself for making it this far is a powerful motivator to keep moving forward. It's about making continual progress toward achieving your goals.

Choose to Aim for Excellence

The achievement of excellence is perhaps the most powerful way to strengthen commitment to a goal. When a person or team excels, others are drawn in by that level of dedication. Think of the commitment of professional athletes on the verge of winning it all or, better yet, think of the commitment exhibited by the fans of these teams. Everyone wants to be part of something special, something that goes beyond what is expected to become extraordinary.

You can inspire commitment in yourself and in others by striving for excellence. When you achieve remarkable results, you will be roused to continue forward in the pursuit of future achievements.

Own Your Goals

Owning your goals and accepting them as your own is another way to hone commitment. Think back to the pride you took in caring for the first big purchase you made with your own money. Whether it was a car, furniture, a home, a piece of jewelry, golf clubs, bicycle, or the latest advance in modern electronics, you most likely paid more attention to the upkeep of

this piece of property because it belonged to you –
you worked for and earned the item. We appreciate
things more when we have to work for them and
your goals are no exception.

A Conversation with Tom Gay

Entrepreneur and Philanthropist

You do a great deal of philanthropic work in South Africa. Tell me a bit about your involvement there and what inspired you to get started.

For five years now, I've been involved with a philanthropic ministry and community upliftment project in South Africa. Each month, the ministry delivers more than 100,000 meals to hungry people in South Africa's Cape Town.

The idea for the ministry was conceived during a visit to see some of the work that we were supporting financially. During that visit, I fell in love with the people and the culture. As a business person, traveling to South Africa was a unique opportunity for me. I was able to go into a community and be received simply as a person who was coming to help. The people didn't know my history of success in business, which gave me a chance to come in under the radar and get an intimate look at what the people were doing and what their needs were. The people were unable to stereotype us because they didn't know us. This allowed us to learn and evaluate from a very open position.

We continued making visits to the country for several years before founding the ministry. During this time, we made all kinds of relational mistakes with the local people. Many issues emerged: some were our fault, others were cultural, and still others were the result of the people's perception of us as newcomers and Americans. Americans are very individualistic and transactional. We want to do a deal, make a 45-minute phone call, and be done. In South Africa, that's not how things are done. People spend hours, even years building a relationship before they begin working together.

I think there's a richness in the life of South African culture that extends beyond what we are capable of understanding in our environment (in

America). This richness stems from having deeper personal relationships. My wife and I are American, but we have more "deep" friends in South Africa than we have here in the U.S. because we've had to learn to invest in relationships.

We had to walk a mile in the people of South Africa's shoes to show that we were sincerely committed to being in a relationship. After about three years of learning, watching, and building relationships, we decided to make a commitment and really get behind something that has a lasting effect on the community.

How do you feel about the concept of living life with no regrets?
I love the concept, but think it's important to clarify that living with no regrets doesn't mean that you aren't going to do things you wish you hadn't done. Living with no regrets also doesn't mean you aren't going to fail. However, if you never take risks, you're going to fail at life.

I once had a mentor who helped reinforce this principle. I made a bad decision that cost the company about $50,000 (keep in mind that this was 30 to 35 years ago in terms of inflation). After reflecting on my mistake and the damage I had caused, I approached my mentor and said, "I screwed up." He looked at me and asked what I had learned from the experience. Then he said, "I've got two things to say to you about this. One – I've never met anyone so forthright and honest about taking responsibility for their mistakes, and for that reason I really appreciate you and want you on my team. Two – don't ever do it again."

I was probably only 26 or 27 at the time and his response just impressed me to no end. I learned two lessons from the experience. First, you must stretch to reach your goals and be willing to accept the consequences of your behavior. Second, if you're not going to make mistakes, no one is going to want you to be on their team.

How did the choices you made throughout

your career effect where you are today?

I believe my choices have had a very significant affect on my life and have opened up doors that otherwise would have been closed. If somebody says to me, "You can't do something," that spurs me to ask, "Why not?" Time and time again I've taken the negatives people have spoken and turned them into positives. This has led to many breakthroughs, such as starting two sizeable, significant companies that have changed the way business is done in the world today.

I believe that all of my business and life experience was in preparation for my ministry in Africa. There is zero difference in the skill set required to build a company with 10,000 employees and the skills necessary to start a ministry organization that feeds 100,000 people per month. It's the same thing.

What have been the greatest rewards of your choices?

Financial rewards aren't at the top of my list.

Financial success is a result or an outcome of life, not the purpose. Financial success is the result of living a life fully and openly. The greatest rewards that I see are the people who are now prospering in life as a result of my having had time with them. It's the children, business people, and young men and women whom I've encouraged and mentored. The new companies have been started by the people I've gotten to teach and work with over the years who are now earning their own success. It's not about the money – it's about having the ability to show others that they can have an impact and build something.

At the end of the day when you take inventory of your life, your greatest accomplishments are not found in the size of your bank account or the number of cars sitting in your garage. Your greatest accomplishments are the people that you've touched.

Are You Committed To Your Success?

Sure, many people say they are committed to their success, but are they really? When it comes to commitment to your success, there has to be a "no excuses – no exception" rule to back it up. This rule is especially true for entrepreneurs, simply because there is no one to point the finger at should things not work out as planned. As an entrepreneur, you are the one holding the key to your success and no one but you can be held accountable.

Once you make a commitment to something, there absolutely has to be a "no excuses – no exception" rule because that is the only rule that separates the failures from the successes. You must cut all ties to an out, escape or alternate plan, because that will set in your mind that failure is not an option. In other words, when you establish only one direction to go, that is where you will go.

Imagine what would happen if you were to commit to your success only 99% of the time:

> 1% percent of your clients would be unhappy with your product or service and proceed to tell 10 of their friends. Those people would proceed to tell their friends they had a friend that had a bad experience. This could translate

into dozens of lost clients and thousands in lost revenue.

- 1% of your printed marketing materials were published with spelling and grammar errors. This has a devastating effect on any business with a poor perception from the public and potential clients.

- 1% of the time you don't answer your e-mail from a prospective client within 24 hours. You respond a few days later, but learn they have taken their business to someone who responded promptly.

See how much of a difference there is between 99% and 100% commitment? Although 1% doesn't sound like much, reaching 100% commitment at every opportunity is not always easy. The only way to truly hold a reputation for commitment is by consistently demonstrating 100% to each and every task. Once genuine commitment is displayed, your success is inevitable.

There are two rules when it comes to commitment and a sure-fire way to catapult your success, but they only work when you are 100% committed!

Rule #1: 100% Commitment to Achieving your Goals

There may be many opportunities for excuses and exceptions, but under no circumstance do you waver from what you truly desire. Ever.

What do you do if your life doesn't support your goal achievement? In all honesty, there's no easy way around it – some changes will have to be made. Sometimes those changes are easy, and other times they're not, especially when there are others to consider. This is no truer when you have a spouse or significant other and/or children. After all, every action you take has the potential to affect them.

You may have to do some soul-searching and find out if you can make changes that will allow you to commit to your goals while having the least amount of impact to those that will be directly affected. If you choose to commit to achieving your goals, do not settle for anything less.

Rule #2: 100% Commitment to Never-Ending Improvement

The second key is committing to never-ending improvement. You may be better than you were yesterday, but not better than you will be tomorrow.

Taking a humble approach to learning is one of the best ways to set yourself up for success. Use every action and reaction as an opportunity to learn how to do things better next time.

In addition, surround yourself with as many positive role models as you can. Watch, listen, and learn from successful entrepreneurs that have gone before you. What you learn can result in huge shifts in your perception and life.

When you are facing obstacles or challenges, do not allow self-doubt, fear, or frustration to sway your commitment. In fact, during these times it is more important than ever to remind yourself why your goals are important to you. Reconnect with the emotions that are the driving force behind your goals and you'll remember why you are taking the steps in the first place to make changes. Remember, your commitment to your success not only benefits you, but those around you and the world as well.

You must embrace commitment if you wish to reach true success.

Actions for a Life with No Regrets

What goals will you commit to?

_____

_____

_____

_____

_____

What will you do to strengthen your commitment to these goals?

_____

_____

_____

_____

_____

How will you empower yourself to remain committed even when faced with the temptation to succumb to instant gratification?

_____

_____

_____

_____

_____

VII Choose to Believe

"If you believe you can, you probably can. If you believe you won't, you most assuredly won't. Belief is the ignition switch that gets you off the launching pad."

Denis Waitley
Motivational speaker and author

16. Choose to be Motivated

"Desire is the key to motivation, but it's determination and commitment to an unrelenting pursuit of your goal - a commitment to excellence – that will enable you to attain the success you seek."

Mario Andretti
Retired Italian-American world champion
racing driver

Motivation and success are built upon a foundation of belief. In order to truly live without regrets, you must possess belief in yourself, your abilities, and your capacity to make the best choices for your short and long-term future.

By definition, belief refers to a psychological state in which a person holds a premise or an idea that he or she discerns to be true. Belief is similar to knowledge, but is differentiated by a level of stronger confidence and perhaps even of faith in the information.

Plato's early works defined knowledge as a person's "justified true belief," or knowledge that has been proven true according to reason, plausibility, and evidence. One could argue that belief and knowledge are relative to the perception of one individual; however, this is a moot point when you consider that whatever a person chooses to believe will ultimately become their reality, regardless if the belief is "true" or not.

During a Ropes Course event I once attended, the participants and I participated in a great exercise that illustrated the power of our beliefs to influence the outcome of a situation. These courses create experiences for people to build trust, build confidence, overcome challenges, strengthen bonds, and have fun.

During one of the exercises, participants were divided into groups and asked to guess how many drops of water we thought would fit on the face of a penny when administered from an eye dropper. Our group fiercely debated how many drops of water from this eye dropper could possibly be captured on this surface before spilling over the edge. Many members of the group thought only two to five drops would fit, while myself and another person guessed that the penny could hold at least 20 drops and thought more was possible.

We eventually convinced the rest of the team to go along with the theory and submitted 20 drops as our answer. When the other team's guesses were posted, our group's guess was the highest. The other groups teased our "ridiculous" number and thought we were crazy.

The ridicule stopped when we actually tested how many drops would fit on a penny without spilling over the edge. Not only was our guess within reason, we actually got about 36 drops on the penny – 16 more drops than our "ridiculous" guess. Interestingly enough, our group was also able to fit more drops on the penny than any other group during the experiment. Every group got more drops on their penny before spilling over the edge then they guessed. Because we believed that more drops would fit, we were able to push the boundaries and keep adding more than the others believed possible.

Belief Makes You Capable

Think about the impact of this one exercise on your beliefs. If you believe more is possible, could you be capable of even more? YES!

Once you learn more about belief, you can understand why you (and others) are prone to certain patterns of behavior and learn how to minimize resistance and maximize productivity. At its most basic level, belief is the ability to maintain a high level of faith in yourself and your potential to overcome obstacles, regardless of any circumstance you may encounter. When you have a high level of belief in yourself, it leaves no room for doubt, allowing you to develop a keen awareness that has infinite potential and can achieve anything you believe you can. In contrast, lack of belief in yourself results in habitual self-doubt that renders you unaware of your potential and your ability to achieve a higher level of success.

17. Choose Your Beliefs

"Many of our beliefs have been formed and not chosen. Choosing requires questioning our beliefs."

Phil Baker

Author and motivational speaker

What Do You Really Believe In?

To get to where you want to go and be who you want to be, you must understand that your beliefs are the powerhouse of creation. Who you are, as well as who you will become, is determined by your beliefs.

Whatever you believe is what you have created and will create in your life. Show me two different people, each achieving different levels of success, and their reality can be directly traced back to their belief system. A healthy belief system gives you the confidence to achieve any goal you set for yourself, while a weak belief system creates habits that sabotage your ability to achieve your goals.

I attended a convention where the lead singer and songwriter for REO Speedwagon, Kevin Cronin, was being interviewed alongside a number of other musical talents. Kevin told a story about an interview he landed at a very young age with a top music producer in America. Getting this appointment meant everything to Kevin because this producer could literally make people or break people. Kevin brought his demo tape to the meeting and the producer listened to 10 seconds of the first track, and 10 seconds of the second track before saying, "Sorry son, this isn't what we're looking for right now but thanks for coming in."

The music producer listened to less than a minute of this young artist's tape before completely dismissing his work. At this junction, many people would be crushed by the producer's opinion. For a person with a shaky self-belief, the "expert's" estimation that the music was worthless would shatter his dreams of becoming a best-selling artist because he would adopt that opinion as the truth.

After Kevin left the producer's office and got outside, he stopped and looked at the demo tape that the producer had dismissed. Rather than accepting defeat because an expert said he didn't have what it takes, Kevin thought, "Well, this guy's tape player must not have been working."

As it turns out, three of the five songs on that demo tape went on to become best selling songs that you may have heard and know.

Kevin's belief in his talent was strong enough that he chose to believe in his opinion over that of someone he perceived to be a very influential person in the field. He didn't allow what another person believed to limit the belief he had in himself and his music.

People with a high level of belief know their success is inevitable. They *know* they can accomplish anything they set their mind to and they keep moving toward their goals because they understand that anything is possible. People who don't have a high level of self-belief, on the other hand, *hope* some things will be possible.

Successful people *know* they are already successful; while people who struggle *hope* or *wish* they will be successful. *Hoping* or *wishing* will not create success, only *knowing* will create success. You can't know you are successful without a high level of *belief*. To get to where you want to go and be who you want to be, you must *believe* you can achieve anything you desire.

18. Choose to Believe in Yourself In Spite of the Opinions of Others

"If you believe you can, and believe it strongly enough, you'll be amazed at what you can do."

Nido Qubein
Author, consultant, and motivational speaker

Have you ever bought into someone else's beliefs and allowed them to trump your own?

You may have heard others say business isn't going as well as they would like because of the economy or season, or whatever the situation. Many people simply buy into this excuse and accept that business is bad because of external circumstances rather than trying to create their own reality and seeing for themselves if their results can be different in spite of the market or economy.

I know someone who didn't buy into what the media and others were saying about the economy during a recession and he experienced great months and years while others flailed to maintain market share in a "tough economy". My friend was able to thrive in a tough market because he believed in his company's ability to succeed and disregarded the opinions of the naysayers. His business was up 20% when many other businesses were experiencing a significant decline and struggling to stay in business.

When a financial advisor was asked how he made 2008 his best year ever and how he was planning to make 2009 even better, Barry Garapedian said, "It wasn't easy. We just *decided* not to buy into the <u>belief</u> that because the market is bad and the economy is bad that our business *has* to be down."

What would happen to your business if you adopted Barry's belief? How would having this belief impact your life?

19. Building Your Beliefs: Conviction and Desire

"When you believe in a thing, believe in it all the way, implicitly and unquestionably."

Walt Disney
American film producer, entrepreneur, entertainer, and philanthropist

To accomplish your goals, you must believe in yourself. A solid self-belief grows from two things: the *conviction* you have in yourself to accomplish anything you set out to do, and the *desire* to accomplish your goals regardless of your current circumstances.

Choose to Strengthen Your Conviction

Conviction is defined as "that which you are convinced to be true, even if you can't physically see it." When you have conviction that you will succeed you can imagine achieving your goals in your mind and feel the sense of accomplishment in your gut. You have absolute resolve that what you are doing is going to work and that you are travelling on the path to even greater success. Conviction means you keep going because you can see the end results before those results have actually manifested.

Be conscious of what you feed your mind. Whatever gets fed to your mind is recorded in your subconscious and determines your future. If you lack a high level of belief, there is one primary cause: what you have been feeding your brain. Whether the thoughts originate with you or are feedback from others, your beliefs are shaped by the information that is recorded in your subconscious.

Take a look at your life and ask yourself if you are *really* where you want to be. Sure, you may be happy or comfortable, but if you can imagine greater things and aren't where you want to be, continue to have a lot of conviction.

Change what you've been telling yourself or prevent the limiting beliefs from your environment to take hold. The truth may be, if you had the amount of conviction it takes to get you where you want to be – you'd already be there or on the path that was leading you there. So if you aren't there yet, strengthen your conviction and get more solidly on the path you know you should be on so you can experience the life you truly want.

This is where you have to go back to something more than *hoping* or *wishing*. You have to tell yourself that you KNOW all things are possible and that your success is inevitable. Constantly feed your mind with reaffirming statements and thoughts until all doubt has been replaced with belief. If you have days where you begin to doubt yourself, immediately stop what you're doing and read positive affirmations, watch a funny movie, listen to inspirational speakers, or contact your life coach – do whatever you can to refocus your thoughts on your infinite potential immediately.

Choose to Strengthen Your Desire

Desire is the emotional aspect of your goal. Desire is the yearning for what you want to manifest in your life. At its root, desire is really just our natural tendency as humans to gravitate toward happiness; the driving force that keeps us moving toward experiences that produce great-feeling emotions.

Desire is really an emotion that is felt in the gut. You feel emotion in the same place when you get butterflies because you're excited, when you get a jolt from good news, when you feel intense love for loved ones, or when you hug your kids. The energy you feel in your gut in any of those situations is the same place where the desire to achieve your goals must be felt. Building your desire will propel you to even greater personal and professional successes.

When you desire something strongly you will do everything in your power to achieve or receive it. When you make calls to prospects and the response you are receiving is not positive, you don't give up. You change your message, modify your delivery of that message, and do whatever you have to do to achieve the desired result. When you call someone who could do business with you, you emphasize aspects that they care about and highlight how doing business with you will help them achieve their goals. Prospective clients are looking for ways to get to where they want to be – just like you. They desire to be at a certain level of success just like you.

By strengthening your desire and catering to the desires of others, you can build belief and accomplish more than you ever dreamed was possible.

20. Are Your Beliefs Helping or Hurting You?

"If you think you can do a thing or think you can't do a thing, you're right."

Henry Ford
American industrialist, founder of Ford Motor, Co.

Wherever you may be in your life, you are in that place because of your beliefs. When you speak to yourself, what do you say? You may not realize it, but your self-talk is creating your belief system. That belief system is either helping you achieve more or keeping you stuck where you are.

Words are powerful things. The words you speak and those you hear can affect your belief and your ability to achieve your goals. Do you offer yourself words of encouragement or words of criticism? If you speak words of encouragement you may have some level of confidence and be successful at achieving your goals. However, if you speak words of criticism, you may find that you are unsure and not as effective at achieving your goals as you would like to be.

Many times negative self-talk is derived from the limiting beliefs that people hold about themselves and their abilities.

Limiting Beliefs

Are limiting beliefs holding you back? Many of us have limiting beliefs that we have never recognized as negative. We hold ourselves back without realizing it.

One day, during a coaching call with a client, he began explaining that he needed more referrals to build his business. We talked about possible referral sources and how many referrals he would need to obtain in order to hit some of his goals. We did some simple math and determined that he would need to obtain five referrals per source in order to meet his goals.

Upon hearing that number, the client's limiting beliefs kicked in. He said that target wouldn't be possible – the number was too big.

When I asked him why he thought that this goal was unrealistic, he said that he typically only receives two referrals per source. I then asked him how many referrals he expected to get. After a moment of hesitation, he timidly responded "Two." So, he expected to receive two referrals per person asked and he actually received two referrals. Interesting!

We all have some limiting beliefs that we don't even realize are holding us back. How might your beliefs be helping you or hurting you? What has to happen for you to change beliefs that could be preventing you from achieving even greater successes in your life?

Limiting beliefs create obstacles to goal achievement. Although limiting beliefs are only thoughts, they do have power over what happens in our lives. When you let go of limiting beliefs, you gain the power to not only get around obstacles, but also prevent your mind from creating them in the future.

The bottom line is that life delivers what we expect. Allow limiting beliefs to limit your potential and you will get exactly what you believe you deserve. Do you ever think any slightly negative thoughts about something and then they come true? The reverse works for positive affirmations. If you transform your limiting beliefs into positive affirmations and actually believe in what you desire, you can manifest that belief into reality.

Changing your circumstances and creating the life you *really* want starts with creating a high level of belief that allows you to feel that you can achieve anything you set your mind upon. With conviction and desire, you will be unstoppable because you believe your goals are possible. As a result, you will create the life you have always dreamed about living.

"What you believe you can do is actually less than what you are capable of."

Bill Bachrach, CSP, CPAE
Author, speaker, business coach, entrepreneur

A Conversation with Tom Voccola
Leadership Consultant and Author

In your book, *The Accidental CEO, A Leader's Journey from Ego to Purpose*, you touch on Limiting Beliefs as a stumbling block to personal and organizational effectiveness. In your experience, have you found some limiting beliefs to be harder to change than others?

From my perspective, the toughest, most resistant limiting beliefs fall into the category of "blind spots."

Sometimes, the obvious is hardest for us to see. This is especially true with our blind spots — points of view, ways of being, issues, and solutions that others might see clearly, but are either invisible to us, or we stubbornly refuse to believe.

Everyone has blind spots, of course, but the most damaging to us are the unacknowledged limiting beliefs that exist within ourselves, our families, and our organizations.

Limiting beliefs have many origins: cultural, religious, social, and experiential. And curiously, every organization, social group, and family develops its own unique set.

Some common examples of organizational limiting beliefs include:
- *We have to put up with bad attitudes from star performers.*
- *It didn't work in the past, so it won't work now.*
- *There's no way we can get the money, so why even bring it up?*
- *Management never listens.*
- *Employees will slack off if left to their own devices.*
- *The only way to improve margins is to cut costs, programs, and staff.*

Any one limiting belief can hold your organization back from reaching its full potential. Yet, the fact is, there are a multitude of limiting beliefs that exist at every level.

Let's take one of my examples. What are the implications of the limiting belief, "Management never listens"? Right now, it is not only sapping energy and enthusiasm from employees, but it is stealing countless innovative ideas from our organizations – innovative ideas that could quite easily counter another limiting belief, "The only way to improve margins is to cut costs, programs and staff."

The challenge is, in order for our organizations and families to see and address their blind spots, we, as leaders, must first choose to be vulnerable and acknowledge our own.

Get some feedback and be brutally honest with yourself. What are you not seeing? Not admitting? Is there anything you don't want to

hear, or that you stubbornly refuse to accept?
What assumptions have you never questioned?

At your next staff meeting (or family gathering), I encourage you to ask each individual to take a moment and write down at least two limiting beliefs of YOURS and THEIRS that they feel are holding the group back. Obviously you will need to ensure a safe space and genuinely commit to no reprisal. Then go around and post each contribution on a flip chart.

Whether or not you agree with what comes up, do not discount anything or respond with "I knew that!" Be generous with your appreciation. Work with the group to prioritize the most destructive limiting beliefs, both yours and theirs, and then agree on a specific plan to address them. Then celebrate! By having the courage to act with authenticity and awareness, you just eliminated a blind spot!

How has this practice of uncovering limiting beliefs affected your ability to live a life with no regrets?

In my early days as a young husband and brash advertising entrepreneur, I used to rely on bullying and bluster to shut down the slightest opposition to my ideas and decisions. My two ex-wives can attest to that.

At the time, I was certain that they were wrong and I was right. That it was their loss, not mine, when things inevitably fell apart. It took a courageous young man who saw the promise behind the personality to get me to a workshop that opened my eyes to my defensive way of being. That experience changed my life. I became dedicated to personal development and examining the relationship between my protective human Ego and my God-given purpose.

Over time I began to distinguish a consistent link

between my external results and my internal belief structure, and I developed a method of guiding myself, and then leaders and their organizations, through a focused process of healing negative issues by shifting from limiting/disempowering beliefs to empowering beliefs. The bottom line when there is a chronic or recurring issue in your life that disturbs your peace, there is a corresponding limiting/disempowering belief linked to it. Locate that belief and intentionally _choose_ to reassign your perspective to an empowering belief, and the issue disappears. Bringing people, especially leaders, to a place of peace within themselves is now what my life's work is about.

I am certainly at peace with the entirety of my life, including my past wife experiences. I've gone back and apologized to each person I am conscious of having wronged, appreciating them and our relationship for giving my life the meaning and depth that it now has. Importantly, early on, I forgave and accepted myself.

We can all live lives of peace and joy without regret. Just pay attention to your wake-up calls when they come and don't shoot the messenger. It takes tremendous courage to be the one to hold up the mirror to someone else's blind spot, to tell the emperor (s)he has no clothes. But I assure you, behind every Ego mask is a worthy purpose and a magnificent soul. And the most rewarding beliefs to unmask are your own.

21. *Choose to Change Your Beliefs and Change Your Life*

"Change comes from within. When you believe in yourself, you can change your life."

Kerri Kelly

Yoga Instructor

There is nothing beyond your reach if you believe in yourself and your abilities. The truth is there is no such thing as you *can't* – you only *think* you can't. Success is not a special privilege handed out to a selected few. Success comes from applying success-oriented beliefs. Transform limiting beliefs into success beliefs and you can achieve anything.

Success beliefs help you realize that you can do anything and any obstacles you face are only imaginary blocks created by your limiting beliefs.

In the next section, you'll learn to tear down limiting beliefs by replacing them with seven success beliefs. There is a science to success and once you learn the truth you will be unstoppable.

The Seven Success Beliefs

1) Success Belief: Everything begins and ends with me

Blaming others for anything, including your reality, is nothing but a limiting belief. What other people say or do does not matter. The only things that count are what you say or do. Everything, good and bad, can always be traced back to an action (or reaction) you made.

Being accountable and taking responsibility for everything in your life isn't just about accepting personal blame. Responsibility is an understanding that you are the creator of your life and you have the power to make successful choices. The power of choice takes you from being a passive acceptor to an active creator.

What new and different choices will you now make?

2) Success Belief: Yes, I can

Self-defeating talk is disempowering – give it up. This negative self-talk literally sucks away all of your creation power. The truth is that there is no such thing as *can't* in most circumstances, although certain tasks may be difficult or challenging. For example, you can be an athlete, dancer, race car driver, golfer, or successful business owner if you chose to set your mind to this goal. It's unlikely you would become a professional athlete without training or experience and probably some genetic assistance, but you *can* be an athlete, dancer, race car driver, golfer, or successful business owner with training and persistence.

Notice I said, *unlikely*? I didn't say *can't* because, really, almost anything you put your mind to is possible. There is no *can't* about it – you *can* if you choose. See the difference? Get back in the driver's seat and speak empowering words like, *I am, I will,* and *I have.* Granted, you have to be more than willing to do the work – you actually have to do the work required. Saying *I am* will not magically transform you into someone else.

3) Success Belief: I am committed to my goals

If you want something, you must actually do the work in order to get it. Commitment requires that you truly desire something. Choosing to do something because someone else wants you to do it only makes it easier to quit. Achieving your goals isn't always hard, but it does take focus, commitment, and work. Commitment is much easier when you have the desire for the end result.

215

Look beyond the goal and you will achieve it. For example, consider a person who breaks bricks with their hand. They don't think about hitting the top of the first brick. They look beyond the bricks and hit through them. When a boxer hits a punching bag, they don't look at the punching bag itself, they look beyond and think about hitting **through** the bag. If you just look at hitting the object, you can physically get hurt. When you look beyond your goals and visualize the desired result, you put yourself in a position to achieve so much more.

4) Success Belief: I believe in myself

From now on, you must believe you can do anything because you realize that success just comes down to applying the right belief system. Those who believe create the impossible every day all over the world. They dissolve disbelief in others by defying the odds and accomplishing what was said to be "the impossible". How did they do it? Because they believed they could do it, and committed to doing what needed to be done to get there. If someone else can achieve the "impossible" – so can you.

5) Success Belief: I will ignore negative talk

Many times you don't even realize the people around you are holding you back. They may not realize they're doing it either. It's human nature for those close to you to want you to remain at their level and keep close relationships. Without realizing it, they are holding you back – and you are allowing it.

If you want something more than you currently have, and realize that means having to loosen the ties with those who are holding you back – you are entitled to excel to your next level. You don't have to necessarily leave these people completely behind, but realize you are not obligated to remain in your current circumstances just because others have trapped themselves at a limited level. You have the freedom to reach the next level, even if your current friends and family choose not to rise with you.

The people around you may mean well, but they don't always say the right things (this includes friends and family). They give us advice because they think they're helping us, but sometimes cause more harm than good. If people around you are telling you that you can't do something – don't listen to them.

6) Success Belief: I will make positive affirmations

Your belief system shapes your reality, so say what you want and state it in the positive. For example, say, "I want a job that unleashes my potential," instead of, "I don't want another mindless job," or, "I want to own my own business," instead of, "I don't want to be stuck in this job forever."

Think about what you want, not what you don't want. Do you think Bill Gates spent all his time thinking about being a college dropout? No – he was too busy being focused on building his multi-billion dollar business.

7) Success Belief: I will take responsibility for my finances

If you want success, you have to learn to manage your money well. If you are in debt, do what you can to reduce or completely eliminate it. If you're on a budget, don't buy new clothes or electronics if you need to pay bills.

Success comes to those who make financial decisions that support their long-term goals and success. Buying a new pair of shoes or a new golf driver is great when you have the money, but if you have $100 in the bank it's just not a decision that supports your success.

Actions for a Life with No Regrets

What limiting beliefs are preventing you from
achieving your true potential?

_____

_____

_____

_____

_____

What reaffirming beliefs could you substitute in place
of these limiting beliefs?

_____

_____

_____

_____

_____

How do you plan to strengthen your reaffirming
beliefs (i.e. a goal board, note card reminders, obtain
feedback and input from others, listen to positive
thinking programs, hire a coach, etc.)?

_____

_____

_____

_____

_____

22. How to Get the Most Out of Life and Live with No Regrets

Are you living life to the fullest? If life ended tomorrow would you feel as though you lived it with no regrets? If you are like most of us, you still have that "someday" list of dreams that haven't yet come true tucked away somewhere.

Life doesn't have to be that way. Be one of the select few that have the philosophy of life figured out and live life without regret. You know, the kind of people that seem at peace, move at a comfortable pace, and don't seem to be distracted by the small stuff. They accept others without judgment and walk with an open heart while the rest of us get caught up in the rush of daily life with no real connection to ourselves or anyone else.

Many of us are so busy that we don't even have time to think about what's missing, let alone trying to figure out how to get the most out of life. What if the solution to living with no regrets was as simple as a single question?

Let's say you had all the financial resources you would need to live the kind of life you have always wanted without having to "work". Would you still be doing what you do every day?

Just for a moment, imagine what you would rather do with your time – the long hours you used to spend in the office. If you can imagine a different life you are probably not getting the most out of life.

Maybe it's time you did. Here are some ways you can begin to change your life and to get the most out it!

Do Something You Love at Least Once a Day

Don't wait one more day to do something you have always wanted to do. Book your reservation to go skydiving, go back to school, write that book, take a road trip, play hooky from work, and take the kids to Disneyland, invent that new product, attend the US Open or some major sporting event – whatever it may be – and commit to doing it. If something simpler is what you really want, that's okay too. Take a bath, read a book or magazine, watch your favorite movie, take a yoga class, visit a friend, go to the driving range, plan a sunset picnic, or even sleep an extra hour per day. Pick something you love to do and make the time in your schedule to do it.

Create More Personal Quality Time

Use moments throughout the day to create thoughts that will positively influence your life. If you are sitting in traffic on the way to and from work (or your place of business) use the time to channel your thoughts to things you would like to experience. For instance, instead of wasting time stewing over something that made you angry, let it go and focus on thoughts that make you happy. The more time you spend visualizing the things you want, the more positively you influence your future.

Create More Shared Quality Time

When you're with family and friends make an effort to leave business out of the discussion, unless there is a valid reason to bring it up. Spend quality time talking about the things that really matter and connect with the people who matter to you most.

Build a Legacy

At the end of your life, what would you like people to say about you? What would you like to leave for your children? If you could change anything for the better, what would it be? When you're not feeling motivated to get the most out of life, think about the personal footprint you will leave and what you would like it to provide. Build a legacy not for the fame, but for the benefit it will provide for those living well after you're gone.

Live with Faith, Not Fear

At first glance it may seem that the average life span of 77 years is a long life. In reality, that time can go by so quickly. Do not waste one moment living in fear because that only scares you out of living life to the fullest. Life is meant to be lived, not passed by. Quit standing on the sidelines – get in the game! What is the worst that can happen?

Now that you've learned how to live life with no regrets, take some time now to create a list of things you'd like to do by life's end and create a game plan to accomplish each one so you can enjoy what is truly important to you in life. Start today!

Regrets are a waste of time – you can't change the past. Live your life with no regrets from this day forward. Remember, taking "baby" steps is perfectly acceptable.

Happiness is a choice. You can choose to live the life you are living or you can choose to live the life you truly want to live. You have the power to choose everything you do in life. What is your choice?

Index

About the Author

Anne M. Bachrach is the president of A.M. Enterprises and a successful Accountability Coach. For nearly a quarter of a century Anne has worked to help business people and entrepreneurs improve their productivity, profitability, and quality of life. Anne inspires her clients to reach their maximum potential. Her coaching is in high demand and she only works with clients who are truly serious about achieving all of their goals and living their dreams.

During her successful IBM career, Anne created training materials and delivered many training programs to clients. She also conducted many executive briefing sessions for top executives.

Anne discovered the benefits of personal accountability while helping her husband build his business. As the revenue generator, marketing person, legal department, and part-time coach, Anne found that she needed to be as efficient as possible to keep up with her workload. She created simple tracking forms to help her stay focused and accomplish the daily tasks necessary to achieve her goals. Her efforts paid off, bringing her husband's revenue from $250,000 to $1,500,000 in a short time.

Anne believes that the first step to true effectiveness is to put systems in place, execute them, and then continuously revise the systems to make them better. Anne says that having someone to answer to on a regular basis about your progress is a powerful motivator. She believes that personal accountability is the single most powerful tool to help professionals improve their businesses and overall quality of life.

Anne prefers to give her clients convenient access to professional guidance and support. She communicates via e-mail and schedules regular follow-up telephone conversations that allow clients to check in, report progress, and get answers to their questions. Her fresh approach to business is a much-needed change for stagnant businesses. Anne coaches sales people to avoid getting stuck in "bad" or traditional habits and to continually think outside the box.

Jokingly nicknamed "The Accountability Pit-Bull", Anne has firmly established her position as the country's foremost expert on Accountability Coaching. She believes that even the most motivated business professionals need guidance to achieve their highest potential. Anne's personal brand of motivational support has helped inspire many business professionals around the country change the way they approach every aspect of business and life.

Aim for what you want each and every day!

Anne M. Bachrach
The Accountability Coach™

www.AccountabilityCoach.com
www.AccountabilityCoach.org

More Praise for Live Life with No Regrets

"I really love your book! One of the highest of all human values is to be able to live your life with no regret. This fabulous book is filled with wisdom and advice for guiding you to make the most out of your life!"

–Thomas Moore
Entrepreneur and Values-Based Financial Planner

"I felt like you wrote the book just for me!"

–Jeani Stevens
CBS Television, Business Development

"What I like best is that the book is brief, to the point, and very actionable. It reflects Anne's direct style which I find refreshing. This book is definitely a must read for anyone who wants to accelerate their results."

–William S. Hart, CFP, MBA
Retirement Strategies, Inc.

"If you have a burning desire to do something and you can't find a way to make it happen, you have to read this book! Regret is defined as "feelings of sorrow, disappointment, or dissatisfaction." Anne's book will guide you towards a life of greater joy, fulfillment, and satisfaction. You will enjoy the practical tools that allow you to start your life changes immediately so you begin your journey of living a life with no regrets from this day forward!"

–Dr. Renee Stetkevich,
Doctor of Physical Therapy and Orthopaedic Certified Specialist

"Do not wait until you are faced with a life-altering event to make positive changes in your life. Anne's book is a field manual to putting your priorities in the right place to improve health and success in all of your endeavors."

–Cathy Herrick Spencer
President, San Diego Historic Properties, Inc.
Breast cancer survivor

"Anne has put together some basic principles and concepts to maintain balance in your life and keep achieving in business and personal life. Along with reinforcing good habits, it will increase your productivity and keep you focused on your goals."

–Mike Sapien
Author, Business Mentor & Technology Adviser

"Where was this book 30 years ago so that I might not have so many regrets? The choices we make do impact our lives in many ways. Making smart choices and not dumb choices you will regret later will save a lot of precious time we don't want to waste. You'll want to choose to read and implement the ideas in this book to help you."

–Rod Carson, CLU, ChFC, CFP®

Spectrum Wealth Advisors, Inc.

is an independent firm

"If you want to live a life with no regrets, this is the book for you! Simple and sensible concepts that can be quickly implemented. Grab a copy of this book for yourself and any other business people you care about."

–Brian Fricke, CFP

author of *Worry Free Retirement*

Named Top Financial Planning Firm

– Orlando Business Journal

"Anne has compiled a menu of great principals and concepts to live by. Anne is a "no non-sense" friend and writer who executes and lives by what she preaches. This book is a unique "invitation for change" to make a difference in people's lives through empowerment by information and choices of strategies to make it possible. Thank you for your choice to share the concepts in this book with us."

–Yousef Ghandour
PT, MOMT, FAAOMPT
Physical Therapist, Clinic Director and Educator in the field of Orthopedic Manual Physical Therapy

"Living without regrets shows us how to achieve the results we want. Living life without regrets helps us look at the big picture to make sure we're leading the life we want to lead. The exercises are valuable and the concepts are powerful. Anyone who reads this book will get a lot of value."

–Ariel Acuña
LTG Capital LLC

"Love the book! While much is written on finding purpose, goal-setting, etc., very little attention seems to be focused on how you actually accomplish what's important. Anne brings her real-world experience as The Accountability Coach™ to provide illuminating examples and great tools to help people make the choices that will improve their lives on a variety of important fronts. Thank you for writing this book."

–Donn Sharer, CFP, ChFC, CLU, CLTC
Sharer & Associates LLC

More Learning Resources from The Accountability Coach™:

- *Excuses Don't Count; Results Rule* – e-book, MP3 audio, and paperback
- *Excuses Don't Count; Results Rule* 34-Lesson Course – e-book
- *Live Life with No Regrets* – e-book, MP3 audio, and paperback
- *Inspirational Quotes for a Balanced and Successful Life* e-book
- No Excuses! Fool-Proof Strategies for Quickly Getting Results Program
- 10 Power Tips for Getting Focused, Organized, and Achieving Your Goals Now!
- Keys to Working Less, Making More Money, and Having a More Balanced Life Special Report
- *The Roadmap to Success* book – Anne contributed a chapter in this book along with Stephen Covey and Ken Blanchard
- *The Middle-Class Millionaire* book by Russ Alan Prince and Lewis Schiff (Anne was interviewed and included in Chapter 6 – The Best Advice Money Can Buy)

Goal Achievement Programs:

- 30-Day Goal Achievement Self-Study Program
- 12-Week Goal Achievement Self-Study Program
- 90-Day Goal Achievement Group Coaching Program

One-on-One Accountability Program:

- One-on-one Accountability Coaching with Anne

Other Programs:
- A Myriad of Tele-seminars
- Half-day and Full-day Training Programs
- Company Group Coaching
- Support Team Coaching
- Membership Programs
- Custom Group Coaching

Other Resources:
- Am I Coachable? Assessment
- The Right Life Balance Assessment
- Wheel of Life Exercise
- Quality of Life Enhancer™ Exercise
- Implementation Index
- What is an Accountability Coach? Booklet
- A variety of articles
- iTunes Podcasts
- Youtube Videos
- Timely News – Spot On… e-newsletter

http://www.accountabilitycoach.com

Anne M. Bachrach

A.M. Enterprises

La Jolla, CA 92037

Anne@AccountabilityCoach.com

858-456-0160 telephone

858-456-0158 fax

ORDERFORM

Name _____

Shipping Address_____

City_____State_____Zip_____

Phone_____

Email _____

Visa ____ MC____ Am Express____

Card #_____

Exp_____ Card Security Code _____

Product   Price

_____   _____

_____   _____

_____   _____

_____   _____

_____   _____

_____   _____

_____   _____

_____   _____

_____   _____

_____   _____

_____   _____

_____   _____

Fax to: 858 456-0158

Please call 858-456-0160 or email
Anne@AccountabilityCoach.com
if you have any questions.

Total   _____

Shipping   _____

CA Tax   _____

Grand Total _____

ORDERFORM

Name _____

Shipping Address_____

City_____State_____Zip_____

Phone_____

Email _____

Visa ___ MC___ Am Express___

Card #_____

Exp_____ Card Security Code _____

Product   Price

_____   _____

_____   _____

_____   _____

_____   _____

_____   _____

_____   _____

_____   _____

_____   _____

_____   _____

_____   _____

_____   _____

_____   _____

Fax to: 858 456-0158   Total   _____

Please call 858-456-0160 or email   Shipping   _____
Anne@AccountabilityCoach.com   CA Tax   _____
if you have any questions.   Grand Total   _____

All prices are in USD

CA tax applies to physical products

http://www.accountabilitycoach.com

Anne M. Bachrach

A.M. Enterprises

La Jolla, CA 92037

Anne@AccountabilityCoach.com

858-456-0160 telephone

858-456-0158 fax

Comments and feedback are always welcome. Let us hear from you on how else we can assist you so you can achieve your goals and enjoy what is truly important to you in life.